MAF

MAPPILLAI

An Italian *Son-in-law* in India

CARLO PIZZATI

**SIMON &
SCHUSTER**

London · New York · Sydney · Toronto · New Delhi

A CBS COMPANY

First published in India by Simon & Schuster India, 2018
A CBS company

Cover photo-portrait of the author in Paramankeni, TN, by © Tishani Doshi
Back cover photograph 'Bagheera on Bagheera beach' by © Carlo Pizzati

1 3 5 7 9 10 8 6 4 2

Simon & Schuster India
818, Indraprakash Building,
21, Barakhamba Road,
New Delhi 110001

www.simonandschuster.co.in

Paperback ISBN: 9789386797162
eBook ISBN: 9789386797179

For sale in the British Commonwealth of Nations only.

Typeset in India by SÜRYA, New Delhi

Printed and bound in India by Replika Press Pvt. Ltd.

MIX
Paper from
responsible sources
FSC® C016779
FSC www.fsc.org

Simon & Schuster India is committed to sourcing paper that is
made from wood grown in sustainable forests and
support the Forest Stewardship Council, the leading
international forest certification organisation.
Our books displaying the FSC logo are
printed on FSC certified paper.

To my mother Editta,
who taught me how to stay safe in the storm.
To my wife Tishani,
who brought me love and serenity.
And in memory of great-uncle Ottone,
who lived in India 70 years ago.

Contents

Life on Bagheera Beach

Dravidian Days

HOW TO BECOME A REVERSE COCONUT

HERE COMES THE GROOM:
LOVE AND MARRIAGE GO TOGETHER LIKE
BULLOCKS AND CARRIAGE

Life on Bagheera Beach

Landing in India for the first time during a most
disastrous year and getting settled as a foreigner,
while exploring spirituality and planning a wedding
in Tamil Nadu's bureaucracy. But…why am I here
leading 'an uncommon life' in an isolated villa on
the beach, among scared snakes, sneaky rats, loud
frogs, and stray dogs?

I don't know what's good for me

Or how the woman who forgot having met me changed my destiny

Life in paradise is full of fragrances. On winter days, the sands reek from the fishy stench of putrefying corpses of seasonally beached turtles, tossed back into the salted water from high-sea trawlers that drown them in their nets.

Olive ridleys are found by fishermen who cut the webbing and set the cadavers to float onto the shore. They slowly rot away at my feet, munched on by crabs and crows, sometimes chewed by dogs. Dead bodies feeding live ones.

The day my father died, on a recent Valentine's Day, I remember I counted five turtle carcasses and a dog's skeleton picked clean by crabs.

After a while, even dried up palm tree leaves can resemble the chest of a skeleton half swallowed by the sand. The seaside is, at times, a place of death, or of transformation, if you choose to look at it at a molecular level.

To distract me from these thoughts, there's the Pye-dog's puppy morning breath, as he jumps to greet me while the sun climbs up in the sky above the horizon. All around me, the low sounding 'hoop-hoop-hoop' of the coucal, the jungle cuckoo of light forests, the occasional rockabilly bulbul, the three silly parakeets, the dancing white egrets, the show-off kingfisher and the narcissistic drongo, as they all come to dance around here, overcome by the pushy common bespectacled mynahs, the sad grasshopper hunters, as they are called.

While I gaze into the dawn, I can smell the frangipani flowers blossoming in the distance while I contemplate the gleaming green of the beach plum and the samba party of the bougainvilleas, as the cacti I lined up meticulously, surrounding them with circles of granite rocks, get swallowed up seasonally by weed, from which the date and coconut palm trees escape safely. Weed is also the worst enemy of my juicy tomatoes, plump pumpkins, stringy green beans, tasty okra, pungent kefir limes, hopeful banana trees, and fragrant lime basil.

I keep plucking these weeds from the wild roses I miraculously transplanted here, blossoming in their delightful shades of yellow, pink, and red. When they grow big enough, I clip them and they keep me company in a glass on my desk.

There's a pretty yellow one, right on the other side of this computer screen, while I'm typing these words.

No one believed my roses would survive this close to the sea and in such corrosive salted air.

Many locals also thought I wouldn't last here.

But I have.

A frontier between two worlds

When I was in my twenties I loved to rock climb. I had ropes, carabiners, and special rubber shoes. I'd inch up the side of a rock slab, high up on the peaks and perch myself into a nook of the mountain to look out into the distant plains.

I could gaze at the world for hours, heart filled with wonder and love for existence. It was as if the mountains were the present I belonged to, and the distant view, the plains of the Veneto, the Adriatic Sea at the horizon sparkling in the sunlight at dawn, or a Mexican desert painted pinkish at sunset, those ancient Peruvian green hills seen from the Machu Picchu, or the sprightly Yosemite forest, collectively represented a future that needed to be perused before being conquered. It was inspiring.

A few years ago, I visited an astrologer. It was not a japamala-rosary peeling sadhu nor a wise Indian man in exotic robes, but a polite, bespectacled and gracious mature lady in my mother's city—Vicenza—in Italy.

Carla Galvan had a computerized system, an algorithm of sorts which she combined with her intuition. And in those years, when I had not yet left for India, she saw that soon in the panorama of my future, I would be surrounded by the colour green for a few years.

I was living in the ancient capital city of Rome at the time, and travelling a lot between a few continents.

I had no plans to move back to the countryside. So I really couldn't picture what she was forecasting.

'Yes, you'll be living surrounded by green,' she insisted, addressing my skepticism, 'I envision green everywhere around you. I can't see more than that.'

I often think of that chromatic prophecy, now, encircled as I am by all this vegetable lusciousness and, beyond, the immense sea.

What that Italian astrologer could not tell me about how I would land here to live out my viridescent years, is that it would all happen because of a woman.

I'm here for love.

Love for a woman who, at first, forgot having met me.

*

In December of 2008, I landed in Chennai, India, after spending a very feverish Christmas all alone in a small hotel in Pondicherry.

It was my first time in India. I'd reached the coast from the city of Tiruvannamalai, after three weeks of barefoot holy pradakshina walks and ashram meditations during a Deepam, a full moon religious festival of lights.

I arrived in a nondescript hotel facing a very drab alley in downtown Chennai, a city I found unimpressive compared to Mysore or Tiruvannamalai, or what I'd seen of India until that point.

I had come to put a pin on the map, but also to meet

a friend of a friend. I knew a translator from English to Italian who'd lived a few winters in India, mostly in Mumbai. 'Lambuji' was her Hindi nickname, meaning the tall one.

Gioia Guerzoni had translated a novel called *The Pleasure Seekers* by a writer, poet, dancer who lived in Chennai. Gioia suggested I email her. The poet said to meet her in the gardens of a theatre across the city— 'Spaces'—down on Elliott's Beach, in the neighbourhood of Besant Nagar.

A rowdy auto-rickshaw driver, after many bumps and sudden breaking and accelerating, finally deposited me in front of the gate of a place that turned out to be one of the most important gardens of my life—the courtyard where I was to meet a stranger who became my wife and the very same place where the two of us would end up celebrating the first day of our wedding six years later.

I'd seen a picture of Tishani on the book jacket of a collection of short stories written by new Indian voices. So, I scanned the crowd of sari-clad young ladies in order to find her.

That's when I spotted the shiningly most charismatic one of the group. I couldn't believe she was so attractive. Forget about that cute young girl still blessed with some baby fat in the photo, I was looking at the most beautiful woman in the world. Forgive the cheesiness—something I'm regularly accused of by that very same woman, but this is actually what I thought.

I also concluded, knowing my own impulsive romantic inclinations, that it was so damned humid in this town that I couldn't possibly allow myself to fall in love with this young lady despite the ebullient storm building up in my bloodstream and lungs and stomach upon seeing her.

Maybe it's not her, I told myself. And, in a way, because of all the sweat pouring out of me on this humid night on 30 December 2008, I cowardly hoped it wasn't her.

I thought I'd give her a missed call to see if she looked at her phone, confirming that it would be one of those evenings in which I was Ulysses tied to a mast tree, crossing rough waters infested with sirens luring me to jump in the dizzying whirlpool to join them.

She did look at her phone. And again I thought: 'I can never move to a place like this, it's too suffocatingly hot here!'

She now says this was an arrogant thought on my part. I maintain that my yogic powers were so enhanced that I had a flash of reverse prophecy, considering how things developed.

The evening was a celebration of her guru and choreographer who'd died two years before. A dance performance in honour of a dancer.

I remember feeling such a warm, welcoming presence next to me, sitting on foldable plastic chairs in the open air at Spaces. I would capture her presence to my right, with my side-view, without looking at her directly, for fear that if I did that she would realize how desperately I was falling for her while I barely even knew her.

So, I mentally repeated the helpful mantra I'd learned from my meditation teacher and told myself this was caused by the sensorial isolation during three weeks of silent meditation at the feet of the holy Arunachala mountain.

'Be careful who you hang out with when you leave the ashram,' I had been warned by Sergio Peterlini, the teacher. 'Make sure you surround yourself with positive, good people, because you might be prone to absorb every sort of influence.' So I tried to behave without responding to my impulse, which was to fall in love with her right there and then. And in such an objectively unbearable climate!

Much later when my wife and I discussed that evening, we agreed that I'd been extremely successful at making myself invisible for fear of falling in love—which is how we explain to each other what happened next.

I mean, nothing happened, that's what happened. Nothing. The show was over and so we chatted a bit and she drove me back to a taxi stand to ship me off to my hotel.

I did not want to be 'that Italian man', the lover-boy who immediately starts pestering and stalking the lovely

Indian-Welsh heartthrob with emails or calls. So, a few weeks later, once back in Italy, I emailed her a thank you note. 'One month later!' my wife now screams, correcting me.

She answered saying she thought I was indeed supposed to come to Madras (she never could cave into the contemporary Dravidian 'Chennai'), but I never did get to the city, did I?

She had *entirely* forgotten having met me.

'I sincerely apologize,' I answered. 'I was sure I had emailed to the Tishani Doshi I met at Spaces Theatre in Madras on December 30, 2008, for the celebration of choreographer Chandralekha. Obviously, I have written to the wrong email address—apologies and please forgive me for the mishap. All the best.'

So I received a couple of mortified emails back, with the phrase 'I'm so sorry ' mentioned a few times, but nothing more.

Regardless of the humiliation, I could not put that woman out of my mind. But I considered it a missed chance. Forever. Italians have a saying for this: *ogni mancata è persa*. In romance, every missed opportunity is a lost one. I was proved wrong, again.

A year and a half later, I was leading an intriguing life. I was subletting an apartment from an artist acquaintance in Rome, near Campo de' Fiori. This allowed me to see my son Teo regularly, born from a previous relationship, since now I could live about 500 metres from his elementary school.

I'd been hired to write a fascinating screenplay for a movie set in Berlin, a city I'd travel to regularly for field research in the Oranienburg concentration camp. I was also trying to finish my first novel about my hometown, a patricide, a historical riddle in the Vatican Museums, and earning freedom from the legacy of the heavy past of my dysfunctional family.

Tristano, the artist I was subletting from, one day said: 'I remember you saying you know Tishani, right? Did you know she's coming to Rome?'

I immediately emailed her: 'I'm the guy you forgot having met.' I offered to welcome her at the airport, but I only had my motorcycle. We agreed to meet the day after, so I could reciprocate her hospitality in India. We decided to meet in front of the Pantheon. What better setting, right?

I pranced into the illustrious Pantheon Square, chest filled with hope, perusing the cafés to find 'the most beautiful woman in the world'. There she was, sitting at a table with a *caffè* in her hand and next to her...some other Indian guy! Amrish, dammit!

Just a friend. From Delhi. But, obviously, so clearly obviously a suitor.

My normally passive nature in matters of the heart, which had mostly attracted overly complicated women who turned out to be no good for me, dissolved with a jolt. This woman brought out the patient seeker in me. I would pursue the matter; I would not give up right away, as I'd be inclined to do in my usual non-attached sort of way.

I offered to chaperone both of them around.

Amrish really did not stand much of a chance. Not because of my impatient tour guide skills, which are famously next to nihil. But, because I was giving it my best.

And yet, once again, nothing happened in Rome. It was time for yet another lucky coincidence, the third one, to kick in as we both had to travel to a northern Italian city with a breath-taking view of the snow-capped Alps.

We were launching our first books at the Turin Book Fair. I was there to send off into the world my non-fiction journal about travels around the world investigating spirituality and technology. She was launching the translation of her first novel.

My publisher's stall was on her way to the local bar and she'd stop by to see if I wanted to go have a coffee with her. My palpitations increased every time she surfaced through the flow of readers along the isles of the Lingotto former factory, where the salon was held.

I hid that excitement under the cloak of the mantra 'Om Nama Shivaya Om Nama Shivaya'—let my excitement not show too much.

That lead to a dreamy, out-of-this-dimension lunch in a restaurant on the banks of the Po River where, as we talked, flowers kept raining down from the pergola above us.

It was all too much, so I had to say it: 'Too Bollywood! Really. Come on, let's go.'

I mean, I know I'm accused of being schmaltzy, but the industrial city of Turin was out-cheesing me in providing an incredible setting for falling in love.

So we'd walk along the river, talking and talking. I think I even over-played the astrology card, as Tishani has been calling me, ever since, the male version of astrologer Linda Goodman. Yes, Pisces and Sagittarius, great combination, excellent, truly, absolutely, most definitely.

In a bookshop, we found a comic book of Corto Maltese, a sailor-traveller character from my part of Italy who explores exotic lands. Dreamy and sentimental. Which is why on her phone, to this day, my nickname still is Captain Malteaser. Or is it Schmaltz-teaser?!

By that time, the Delhi suitor had shown up in Turin too, unrelenting as only a Dilliwalla can be. And yet, as I played it cool pretending not to have any ulterior motives, Amrish tried to put me down, mocking my Linda Goodman side, with little jabs like: 'How can the entire world population have only twelve types of behaviour? Every day, Carlo? Really? Do you really believe that? Come on…'

Harmless jabs, part of a technique which ended up digging his own grave, tactically. Upon realizing it, he wisely decided it was exit time and off he went to Milan.

Still, it wasn't happening. I'd never been an excessively straightforward, pushy man who gets what he wants and gets it fast. I was interested in the slow development, in the getting-to-know-each-other-and-letting-it-happen-unhurriedly.

This is why, when she travelled to Venice for another literary event, Incroci di Civiltà, I just so happened to feel the need to visit my brother Lodovico, who at the time was living in Venice with his family.

Venice. My city. My turf. I'd always felt like this dream of a city was the real capital of my homeland. And I felt she was finally in my territory, among labyrinthine alleys, lacquered black gondolas, and mysterious canals.

Cutting to the chase scene: we found ourselves on a bench in the Giardini di Sant'Elena, near the Biennale. Children playing on slides and hanging from monkey bars, behind us *vaporetti* gliding by on the *laguna* in a somewhat greyish, mild late afternoon.

My right arm reached over, behind her smooth neck, and rested on the wooden bench. She leaned her head however imperceptibly towards me. The first kiss.

Now that I live in Tamil Nadu with this gift that is my wife, I think of the phrase I told myself when I saw her in that garden at Spaces in Besant Nagar: 'I couldn't possibly move to such a humid climate.'

And I realize how little I know about what's good for me.

Which may be empirical proof that I'm an idiot, or a lunatic.

Although, to pursue my destiny and end up living in the isolated paradise by the sea where I'm writing this, I was asked to first sign a document stating exactly the opposite.

Harsh Sadhaka is no idiot nor a lunatic

Or how I almost got a Hindu name so I could get married

'Sure you can get married in India,' says the Hindu priest. 'You might have to change your name though. If you convert, you join our religion. You join our religion, you get a Hindu name.' The priest is slim and nervous. Seems like there's somewhere else he'd rather be.

'You'll have to change your name,' he says, 'in everything, all your documents, your foreign passport. All!'

'All,' he insists with that typical swing of the hand, five fingers pressed together pointing to him and then, suddenly, swinging out, all, while the hand opens with a swift tilt now spread as if he were sprinkling holy water on a crowd. All!

I'm allergic to the idea of converting to anything. Converting is like joining a group or a cult. Never been a joiner. Schooled in the States, never joined a fraternity. Lived my early years in Italy, never sided with any political party. Didn't even have a favourite football team! Must have gotten off on the wrong foot by not even being christened. What? A non-christened Italian who doesn't root for a football team?

The name I would be surrendering comes from the old Germanic 'Karla', which means 'free man'. How can a free man join a religion, a word that means 'something binding people together and to their vows'?

*

'Most spiritual atheist I know' is how my best friend tagged me—an atheist with a penchant for the mystical. Yet I could never bring myself to take that famous leap of faith, curtailed as I was by a startlingly rational approach.

As a teenager, I'd studied Buddhism, inspired by Herman Hesse's *Siddhartha*...and, yes, I also began dreaming of India. Then, I had to attend the First United Methodist Church in Pensacola, Florida, along with an American family hosting me for a year as an exchange student. In the Bible Belt, I met a few Born-again Baptists. Some were bombing abortion clinics in front of my college. That rid me of any further distant desire to dally with religions!

As a rational adolescent, I worried that if I joined a faith, if I conceived of a God, I would have to devote my entire existence to this Supreme Lord. I would have to become a monk. I felt that if, all of a sudden, I realized that there was indeed a Superior Being, I'd be a fool to continue living my normal, acquisitive life, led by desires, mistakes, successes, but mostly dragged down by failures.

I'd have to detach from all things. Material existence would make very little sense, if there were a God and an afterlife.

*

In India, I have worn rudraksha and Gauri Shankar seeds around my neck. I have memorized the Ganesha stotram. I have chanted bhajans and Om Namah Shivaya, reeling these off while turning a japamala. I have walked barefoot, doing pradakshinas around Arunachala, the mountain which is Shiva. I have asked Ganesh to realize certain hopes.

Could it hurt to try a little irrationality? By the way, the wishes have all been granted.

Sometimes, I visit Hindu temples and meditate in them. I like to think of Shiva and Vishnu and Brahma— or Hanuman, Parvati, Saraswati, Krishna—as being Atman, all pervasive and timeless. If there is indeed a God, it will be everywhere: sounds like a good hypothesis to me.

Will this thought allow me to become a Hindu?

I doubt it.

So, what am I doing here, thinking about changing my name to a Hindu one, so I can get married in India?

That said…just in case I decide to go down this path, I've been searching for a Hindu name. I realize you're supposed to be given a name, and I've been told my date of birth relates to the god Rudra (although some have seen Krishna's roguishness in me)…but, at the very least, I should have options.

And then the name comes to me.

Harsh Sadhaka.

Hello, nice to meet you, I'm Harsh, Harsh Sadhaka.

Hello, Mr Sadhaka?

Yes, that's me, call me Harsh.

I've tested it. Tried it. Even liked it. For a while.

I've chosen Harsh because its meaning in Sanskrit is stridently the opposite of that in English. It is not 'coarse' and 'rough', as I am sometimes accused of being. It means 'joy', 'pleasure'. And a Sadhaka is a 'seeker', a 'student', which I most certainly identify with.

Yes, when I think about it, 'pleasure seeker' seems to me a secular and hedonistic choice for a new name. And it reminds me of the title of a novel…

And yet, when I think about it further, I see this name more as meaning someone who pursues the silent joy reached in meditation—a joy similar to moksha— than that of a wanton drunkard who constantly seeks sensual gratification.

Harsh Sadhaka. Yes. That could be my name if I were to become a Hindu. But am I?

I've tried talking to an Indian friend about this possibility. She says: 'Well, it could also mean "lover boy", are you sure you wanna go with that, being Italian and all?'

*

In the end we opted for the ritual of the Arya Samaj— 'The Noble Society' who rejects worship of idols, professes to believe in equality of all human beings and empowerment of women. Plus, they don't require hinduization of names for marriage. Which meant I got to keep mine.

They have an alluring ritual. Romantic even. You point to a star and you say that's me, the husband, the brighter star. Hmm, empowerment of women? Okay, a bit condescending, even patriarchal, but still picturesque.

Switching to the noble society of the Arya Samaj was not the end or the beginning of it. There was the registration to take care of. Bureaucracy is one of the few words the French contributed to the world which is not fun at all—unlike, say, liaison or croissant.

It's not like I've always wanted to get married or been burning with desire to do it. My girlfriend—the young woman who forgot having met me—at one point during our long engagement, simply told me: 'I think you should marry me. Hello? I'm a caaatch!'

I thought about it for a few seconds and realized she was right. For the first time in my life, I said yes, let's get married.

But I had one condition. It had to be an Indian wedding. If I have to be in a show, it might as well be a colourful one.

She said: 'Yes. Ok, Indian wedding it is.'

I said: 'I want to ride into it like in the Hindi movies.'

'How?' my about-to-be betrothed asked.

'On a horse, what else?'

'No horses in the fishermen's village where we'll get married.'

'On an elephant?' I ventured.

'No elephants in this village.'

'Well, I'm not going to ride a motorcycle!' I blurted out.

So, I ended up riding in as King Carlo on a bullock cart, chanting phrases I didn't understand in Hindi, while wearing an orange turban with a funny little feather on it. The bullock's horns were painted pink.

But let's go back to how we were even able to get married.

Until that moment, until I was propositioned with 'I'm a caaatch,' marriage had been a puzzling country refusing me a permanent visa.

But I'd finally done it. I said yes.

Now we had to go and register ourselves before the four-day marriage ceremony that we'd live to regret. Not the getting married bit, just the organizational worries that came along with it.

One of the major takeaways from the experience has been that the Indian wedding is the result of millennia of wisdom. The long, expensive, exhausting, complex process is designed to teach a basic lesson: once you get married in an Indian ceremony, you'll be so tired you'll never want to go through it again. This may explain the low divorce rate in India compared to countries with hastier rituals.

One of the major hurdles—and another pivotal reason for never wanting to repeat the marriage experience—is called the Registrar's Office.

The Registrar's Office in Chennai is probably representative of all its counterparts in India, but there's always someone ready to steal the Guinness World Records prize—and this particular office might just be THE worst.

Do not take my word for it. Just follow me as we inch our way through a crowded, sweaty and noisy building in downtown Chennai, where my wife-to-be and I, while entangled in hydra-headed bureaucracy, are asked to vouch for the fact that we are not idiots.

Literally.

Our marriage certificate request, Point n. 8 of FORM III (Vide Rule 7a)—whatever that means—spells it out, among typos and dubious grammar: 'We hereby declare that 7. Neither of us has more than one spouse living on the date mentioned in this application. 8. Neither of us, an idiot or lunatics.'

It says that, I'm serious. But, there's more than one problem here.

First of all, Point n. 8 is a contradiction in terms. I've heard several theories regarding the Indian mind and the cohabitation of apparently contradicting truths. It's all for mystical purposes. It's all part of that great lesson India bestows upon supplicants such as my whitey self.

But since marriage is statistically the primary cause for divorce, and given today's divorce rates, it follows that the prerequisite FOR getting married is to be either an idiot or a lunatic.

Of course, what's especially problematic about Point n. 8 of FORM III is that if you are mentally challenged, you are not allowed to marry. Which, if you really think about it, is along the borderlines of eugenics. And we know how that party ended in Germany in the 1940s.

I may be an idiot and a lunatic, but I say it is wrong.

Maybe this is because in the northern Italian city where I grew up I knew a girl we called Miss Smile. She thought she was Marilyn Monroe. She'd walk down the main street in fluffy miniskirts, counting each step taken by her high heels, holding a wild flower bouquet in one hand and clutching an invisible tea-cup in the other.

She met a boy who smiled and looked into emptiness. Nobody thought they couldn't get married. They were a good match because together they were happy. Which is the point, really, of marriage, isn't it? Not being whatever is considered normal. Just being compatible.

Miss Smile and her beau were an unusual match. No more or less unusual than the idiot and the lunatic who moved to a beach house in the south and adopted eighteen stray dogs.

Why I'm in India leading 'the uncommon life'
Or making yourself invisible is not enough to escape fate

'You have made exceptional choices and you've lead an exceptional existence. You have gone to live far from the world. You are living an experience no one else is living. Why don't you face these things head on?'

The Italian editor I'm having a discussion with, Antonio Franchini, is very evidently rejecting the idea of publishing my latest novel, while suggesting I write something else. Antonio goes to *muay thai* kickboxing and judo practice at lunch break. He rivets his intelligent martial arts gaze on you through his thick eyeglass lenses when he speaks with a precise, slightly nasal cadence. Every word is a hit. So you better listen to him.

We're sitting in his open space office, in a gigantic architectural marvel, on the outskirts of Milan, surrounded by an artificial lake. Imagine a vintage '70s Gurgaon in Northern Italy, if you can.

'You are leading an eccentric life. Why not tell it directly? Why does a man your age and with your background decide to go and live in such a remote area of India? It's an uncommon choice, in an uncommon area with an uncommon woman. So I ask myself: what does an Indian fisherman think of an Italian who lives 10 km from his house?' *It's just 1 km*, I mentally correct him, but I keep my lips zipped. He is an editor and, like all editors, hates being edited. Plus, kickboxing...

'I mean, what do you think of him, of the fisherman? What does he think of you? And what do you think, at night, as you stare out into the darkness of the Indian Ocean…?' *It's the Bay of Bengal, man!* My querulous inner editor keeps mumbling in my brain. *It's not the Indian Ocean!*

'Hmm…you want to know what I think about as I look into the darkness?' I ask.

'Yeah, what do you think about?' Antonio says.

'I cry out: why the hell have I still not published a novel with Mondadoriiii?!'

He laughs. Kind of. More of a sneer. Something in the punchline wounds him. He probably would've preferred to see me scream my rage against the wind of that obscure NOT Indian ocean, something more *Sturm und Drang*, more Goethian, than my frustrated writer's whining and whimpering. 'The extraordinary tale of an allegedly extraordinary life' is what he wants from me.

What's so extraordinary? From Antonio's point of view it's probably the fact I've often left what is material behind me. As soon as I'd satisfied my ambition, I'd leave, looking for new challenges. Even before India.

From the age of 16, I've lived in 13 cities before settling in Chennai—set up camp, integrate, work, make friends, then say goodbye to friends, lovers, apartments, jobs, furniture, habits, memories. That's been my *modus operandi*.

Everything ends. Travel light. Avoid the delusion of permanence. Be ready to lose it all.

I don't own the house I live in, I don't own much: dozens of clothes, hundreds of books, three digital devices and a Honda Hawk 650 cc, vintage 1990 motorcycle. (It's for sale.)

Fear keeps many people from letting things go. It leads many, who have enough to live on, to go through existence as slaves of the future.

But this has a price. Sometimes it's called depression. Compromise. Boredom. Anger. Frustration. It feeds on greed for wealth, power or love. It's an anxiety killing you a little at a time, every single day of what may seem a shielded life, until you realize, maybe on your last day, that you are not what you own or what you've acquired, be it position or assets. Not being afraid of losing what or who you think is your property, might get you to live a full life. Extraordinary?

But Antonio doesn't want all this from me. He wants what he thinks is extraordinary. He needs the extraordinary. That sells. The thirst for the extraordinary. This is where we're at today. The constant need for the sensational. Instead of the wise, useful effort in finding what is disquieting in the normal, or what is normal in the disquieting, we're infected with the constant need for the sensational.

This is why we are so accustomed to excitement. And

what we are constantly trying to feed on. Click, click, click. Blame it on social networks, if you're so inclined. But if you have indeed lead an uncommon life, you will see how extraordinary normalcy is.

This is what I have always sought, trying to shade my weirdness under a normal appearance, even though innately driven towards the eccentric.

The tranquility of a normal family—where mother, father, daughter and son sit together at breakfast in harmony, chatting and joking. Some days with a bit of nervous tension, or filled with pure love, with fatigue, some days shaken by the thrill of love for life itself, moments in which even discussing the dynamics of a game of bridge can turn to laughter.

This is what I found in India. Not enlightenment.

Unless this is enlightenment, as it may very well be, in a way.

I've had some adventures, and they inevitably keep lurking around the corner. But in what looks like the exotic land of 'a far away world,' as Antonio defined it since it is far away from him, I've found the calm of family life. As a mappillai in Tamil Nadu. A son-in-law.

This is my wild frontier—a regular life, the golden lining surrounding like a halo the protagonists of my daily life, either in my in-laws' regular two-storey home in the quite regular neighbourhood of regular Besant Nagar, in Kalakshetra Colony near Elliot's Beach in regular Chennai, or in a more barefoot life in a two-stories villa where I live with my wife, an hour and a half south of the city, in a rather isolated thin peninsula, caught between the paddy fields of the Buckingham Canal flowing into Odiyur Lake, and the famous rolling waves of the Bay of Bengal (not the Indian Ocean!), in a shore I've nicknamed Bagheera Beach, after the oldest and most beloved beach dog my wife and I have adopted here.

From that terrace overlooking Bagheera Beach I observe…nothing. Or rather, nothing extraordinary.

It may look extraordinary to someone, like that editor, Antonio, who has to drive out of Milan everyday into what looks like an elegant factory, surrounded by futuristically styled lakes and sculptures, and sits in his cubicle in a dreaded open space. He stares out the window once in a while, into the smog of a polluted, melancholic plain known as the Pianura Padana, something that rhymes and reminds me of Haryana.

I come from those Northern Italian parts. I grew up with that Orientalist craving for sunny exoticism, dictated by the grimness of an industrialized life called development.

But, now, from my terrace on Bagheera Beach, in a house my mother-in-law, Eira, baptized with the Welsh name of 'Ar Lan y Môr' which means 'Beside the Sea', all I observe are goat herders and their goats, Indian barefoot cowboys in their lungis poking their cattle, the occasional construction workers or fishermen running out to the waves to squat, shit, scuttle forward a few steps for a fast 'wave-bidet', put their lungis back up, and pensively return to their daily business. Or the dazed meditators oozing out of the hedge-fund manager ashram up the beach, clad in white kurtas, a relaxed, dreamy smile on their faces.

I hear the constant breath of the waves and the wind, the monsoon rain filling the terrace and trickling down the roof. And in the right season the put-putting of fishing boats, while a devastated carburettor roars into the silence of dawn its scream of ownership of the landscape: humans are here, they are here to capture fish, and they are not shy about it!

I see the palm trees I've planted, the 10 cactus plants into a nice curving row, each necklaced with their own garland of rocks. The fragrant frangipani, the neem bush hiding the dark granite statue of Ganesh I bought in Mamallapuram; the water-sucking casuarina trees that were supposed to protect the soil from a second tsunami, after the 2004 disaster wiped away the foundations of Arlanymor.

I see a squirrel running along the frail brick wall, chased by a hawk or is it an osprey? Egrets seasonally come to dance their reptilian moves in search for scrambled insects for breakfast.

Once, I saw a rat snake swerve around the corner of the house. And also a tree snake chasing a frog across the wispy green grass lawn and then gulp it down.

I've seen 18 dogs, at one point, populate the garden. I've also seen most of them die and only the matriarch Bagheera survive.

I've seen my own wedding filling the wide garden with white tents and cheerful friends from many corners of the world come here to dance or sing, with operatic voices, melancholic Welsh songs.

I saw an acquired Scottish uncle, Chris, skipping and hopping away in his kilt and my new Gujju Jain cousins improvise a most dazzling Bollywood choreography for us all.

And I loved them all.

The Jain cousins, the Scottish uncle, my dear friends and my teenage pale Italian son who'd travel here from Rome to stay with me and wear a lungi and do pooja with the smiling caretaker Ammu at the Ganesh statue, along with my septuagenarian mom, who would walk around in circles around an idol she didn't fully understand, but she wanted to go along with the extraordinary life of this *preferito* son of hers.

I loved them all, the shitting fishermen on the beach, the workers who burned plastic upwind as I ran out to chase them away brandishing a big stick, but mostly armed by all that dad-bod white flesh they weren't sure if it made them laugh or be scared, as if they'd seen the materialization of a vellai ('white' in the Tamil language) Asura.

I loved and love them all. The tree snake I found in the knife rack on the window sill in the kitchen. Not sure who was scared the most. We knew we both were terrified. Both equally dangerous to each other, in our own minds. Nature and man.

And I love the family of toads we allow to live behind our cupboard filled with family crystals my sister and her family brought as my dowry, along with the ancient family porcelain, a piece of the Old Continent brought to the even Older Continent.

The toads eat the mosquitos and the cockroaches. We like to think of them as a more organic solution than rat poison. Which is what I had to finally stoop to, spreading coal-black crumbs on the pantry floor, once I got tired of mice nibbling on my wife's fingertip, a rat dancing on my hip and chewing on my cables, and generically making Broadway entrances in our bedroom or gnawing away at my staple food (bananas!).

I finally had to use that Mashobra walking stick to whack a few of them out of existence, one even in mid-air like an ace batsman, and apologizing either aloud or in my spiritual-atheistic conscience for having taken their lives.

This is the extraordinarily ordinary life I lead. This

is the story of a man already way into his 40s who comes to India for the first time after much fear of this country, goes to study yoga just like any ridiculous Five Fingers Vibram shoes new-age joke you would picture, and then goes meditating in an ashram with a bunch of mantra screaming Italians in Tiruvannamalai, and allows doctor Sambhu to insert an Ayurvedic big ghee enema in the most vulnerable of orifices to study the secrets of Panchakarma. All in the name of book research. All to try and keep that extraordinary life going, in a way.

Inevitably drawn to the eccentric, secretly coveting the normal life of a husband, a mappillai who sits with his father-in-law in the Rukmani Road veranda in Chennai and listens to the stories of a different India, when there was only one TV channel, when getting any product was complicated, the India that slowly begins to understand the absurdity of Ration Cards for everyone, including millionaires, the Bharat that wants to promote a neo-liberal, free-market mentality but is still, technically, a socialist republic lead by a Hindu fundamentalist.

Yes, the good ol' India of contradictions.

I discover it from a much neglected observatory: the South. Tamil Nadu. A world in and of itself, so, maybe, not indicative of the whole country.

But, then, what would be indicative of this diverse identity called India?

There are 11 main ethnic groups here. Hundreds more subdivisions. Half the nation speaks Hindi. But there are the Marathis, Gujaratis, Bengalis, Kashmiris and Punjabis up there in the North with their own language. And down here the Dravidians—the Tamil, Malayali, Telugu, Kannada speakers, and up there again the Assamese, Nepalis, Sikkimese, all the North-easterners with yet another culture. Let's not leave out the Anglo-Indians and the Zoroastrians, the Sikhs, the Parsis, and all the various tribes.

The list never seems to end in a place where you have as many ethnicities as you find in the continent of Africa, all stuffed in a country roughly the size of Argentina.

A unified whole? Not really, because this *topos* of India, the recurring theme, is actually an invention. And thus I can think of no better way to look at this marvellous human experiment called India, than to start from its outskirts.

Not from Delhi, where things are happening; not from Mumbai, where things are shakin'; nor from Bangalore, a city trying to delineate a new matrix for being a young Indian; nor in the up and coming Hyderabad or in languid Kolkata, or Ahmedabad or Lucknow.

No. Tamil Nadu. Where Hindi is not welcome. Where people are still fervently proud of being Dravidian. THE Tamil Nadu, home to Korean and Japanese automobile manufacturers, which has traditionally been, in a way, cosmopolitan, and is very slowly trying to gain back that flavour.

This glocalism is more representative of what is happening in the whole world than the power games of Delhi 'where things are happening'. (Like what? Pollution? Corruption? Power gossip?)

But let's face it, this is all irrelevant, because when the question gets asked, as it does, about why here, why Chennai, why the village of Paramenkeni, the only real answer is cheesy but true: love.

Do I like to give that answer? No. This is what fills the eyes of the literature festival public with romantic joy. But am I embarrassed by it? A little.

I feel I should be my own man. Like a passionate indo-phile who is here because of the lure of an ancient civilization, its supreme wisdom, or the call of the Vedic texts and of Sanskrit, or because India is the next China. Whatever. A more macho reason. A more serious purpose that proves that I'm a real man, thinking and operating on really important things like history, contemporary economics, ancient theology. I dunno, a Wendy Doniger, a Roberto Calasso, a William Dalrymple, a Patrick French, a Herman Keyserling, a Paul Brunton.

I ain't.

I mean, I did come here in search of my own secret

India, the first time I landed in Bangalore in the autumn of 2008. And I did find the deep change and answers us whiteys often seek here. But, mostly, what I found is the woman who'd bring me back here for good.

How Italian of me! How utterly non-masculine, and weak of me. I have no alibi, no excuses, no extenuating circumstances, none that I feel at liberty to divulge here. Not yet, at least.

Trigger warning: this is NOT an India book
...although it kind of is, I know

'Oh, no,' my wife says, 'you are NOT going to write an India book, are you?'

'No, I'm not, I promise.'

This book will not attempt to explain something that cannot be dissected, as it is ever changing.

There are so many Indias. There's a tangible, smellable, real India. There's an imaginary, literary, dreamed India.

Writing about India is like writing about the mafia. It's like owning a pharmacy. Everyone is bound to always get sick, there'll always be a need for medicines. A never-ending, lucrative business.

Whether you want to find out about India's Maximum City, its White Tigers, its Slum-dog Millionaires, its Cities of Joy, or whether India is calling or coming or becoming, whether you want to know about its makers, its prisons or its 50 incarnations or its nine lives, India is there to be told. To be explained and often mansplained.

Not here, not in these pages. Nope. Here you'll have to read about simple, real, one-sided, totally biased and culturally slanted personal anecdotes and opinions from a recovering Orientalist.

But, think about it, hasn't this really been the fate

of all the people who've come for religion or to conquer or for love and have been captivated?

In the end what remains is just the tale of what happened to them.

Facts count not words, people say. Actually, it's the other way around.

Facts disappear, words stay. Words count. Facts go.

I guess it all started with the historian Megasthenes, the first foreigner from the West who wrote about India. He left Greece around 300 BC and, after crossing Anatolia and Mesopotamia, finally reached Lahore and then Allahabad. The first whitey or *gora*, as they're called in Hindi, to tell his side of the story about India and Indians.

Diodorus, Strabo, Pliny and Adrian all plagiarized from his *Indica* (not just a type of cannabis, but also the title of Megasthenes' book). He mixed local legends with personal tales.

This is the first time, in known Western history, a whitey wrote back home about that 'far-away land' where I now live: 'The inhabitants of India are distinguished in their proud bearing.'

Guess not much has changed in 2318 years.

But what about visitors from the East, like Faxian, the Chinese pilgrim scholar who wrote *A Record of Buddhistic Kingdoms* after travelling to India and Sri Lanka in 388 AD? He opened the way for many Chinese scholars who searched for the ultimate truth in the headquarters of spirituality—India.

The many Sanskrit texts he translated and brought back contributed to the strengthening of Buddhism in China. It wasn't trouble-free; he got stranded for 200 days on a boat hitting rough waters.

Travelling to India has never really been simple, nor legal. In 629 AD a very young Xuanzang disobeyed Emperor Taizong of China who, citing threats to national security, had prohibited him from traveling here. I guess China has not really changed *that* much either.

Xuanzang allegedly defeated 500 Hindu, Jain and heterodox Buddhist scholars during an 18-day-long debate. 'Though ordinary Indians are naturally light minded,' he wrote, 'they are upright and honourable.' He must have confused the smiles as 'light minded'.

Descending from today's Uzbekistan in 1019, Al-Biruni reached India and wrote about it after studying the Gita, Patanjali's sutras, the Puranas and the Vedas. 'I thought myself a great deal superior to them Hindus, disdaining to be put on a level with them.'

Then Marco Polo finally got here. The ultimate gora. He comes from my homeland, Venice and the Veneto. The Venetian traveller was only 17 when he reached Kublai Khan's court and got stuck there.

On his way home in 1292, he landed in India with a merchant ship entering the kingdom of the Pandyas, near Thanjavur, a couple of hours drive from where I am now, writing this. On he went to Malabar to describe it for those European readers who soon would love his often discredited *The Million*.

I like to think of him as a pioneer of creative nonfiction. 'So strict are these idolaters and so stubborn in their misbeliefs.'

I know Ibn Battuta is considered more reliable than Marco Polo. He reached here in 1333, as he writes in *My Travels*. He worked as a judge in the court of Muhammad bin Tughlaq in Delhi, before heading to the Mongol court in China.

Domingo Paes is another whitey from Portugal who reached Hampi via Calicut in 1498. He was a horse dealer who traded in his stallions for a pen and authored *The Narrative of Domingo Paes*.

Then you have the Brits. Latecomers, really. Thomas Roe, ambassador to the court of the Mughal emperor Jahangir between 1614–18. In his *Journal of Sir Thomas Roe*, he detailed the India of those years, as seen through his gora perspective, of course. And, by doing so, he paved the way to the East India Company expansion, conquests and massacres. Again, the pen is mightier than the sword.

In 1765, it was the turn of the Abbe Dubois, French educator and priest who left the French Revolution behind him to spend 30 years here on a mission to India to convert Hindus into Roman Catholics.

Oh, I feel for the poor Tamil fishermen having to listen to all his funny-accent sermons. Growing up in the very Catholic region of Veneto and in the Born-Again-Christian Bible Belt on the border with Alabama as an un-christened atheist, I've often had to face many of these proselytisers myself. None succeeded with stubborn me.

Abbe Dubois also finally gave up, convinced that converting Hindus 'with their deep-rooted prejudice' was simply impossible. But at least he persuaded many Indians to get vaccinated against smallpox.

He was hanging out in Pondicherry, before moving to Mysore. A bit of a sourpuss, but hey, he was French after all: 'Intense selfishness is a common characteristic of a Brahmin,' he wrote. I have some friends in Chennai with a form of Tamil Brahmin-allergy who would agree with that.

The Protestants had their go as well, down here. Reginald Heber was a hymn writer and the second Anglican bishop of Calcutta. He tried to spread Christianity, getting sick all the time. And my recurring gastroenteritis can sympathize with that, Bishop Heber.

Chennai's St George's Cathedral was erected in his honour, mostly for having been able to open a dialogue with Hinduism.

Whitey with a mission.

But no, *this* is not an India book. Because I don't know India.

Although I live here, I don't profoundly understand it.

'Sir, that is indeed the first sign that you are beginning to understand it!' says a nasal, Indian twang voice inside my head, which my wife calls my politically incorrect inner Apu-from-*The-Simpsons* voice.

But it is inevitable. As you Indianize, you start getting affected by that Indian ailment called 'obsession for national self-enquiry'.

Dozens of books on India, on understanding, explaining, praising, criticizing, dissecting, and documenting India are a constant publishing success.

How India is becoming India, how India is new, how it's succeeding, how it is failing, how it is inimitable, how it is imitating everyone else, mostly the Brits and Americans.

Blame this latest trend of indology on Sir Vidiadhar Naipaul who started in 1964, continued in 1977, and then had a thousand mutinies to talk about in 1990.

Blame it on Sunil Khilnani and his idea of India, or on how people imagine India, or are calling India; or as some authors, penning short stories or discussing cricket matches, constantly remind readers in their book titles that there are 1.2 billion people here (now almost 1.3 billion, by the way, says the petulant statistician nestled in my mind).

Would it be possible, asked author Amit Chaudhuri, exhausted by this phenomenon, to imitate French writer

George Perec who, following the dictates of the literate gang called Oulipo, was able to avoid the letter 'e' for the entire text of his *La Disparition* (or *The Disappearance*) and could anyone write a book in India, about India, avoiding the word 'India'?

You wish.

Americans, Albert Einstein famously noticed, *are* not, they are *becoming*. And so are Indians. And India. It *isn't*, it is *constantly becoming* something else, which prompted my friend Akash Kapur to title his well-researched India book *India Becoming*, of course. Because India keeps changing, it follows that you have a constant need for India books.

India is obsessed with herself, and while some Europeans still find it painful when non-Europeans discuss their history or politics, Indians so far have welcomed, to a certain degree, the foreign gaze into their reality. Hence, the very same book you're reading.

Yet, the European gaze is so often such a tainted and slanted gaze. If you are Italian, French or German, you are bound to have shaped in your mind a more spiritual and mystical view of India. The India where everyone might be a secret guru.

India, for these mainland Europeans, can be the gateway to a certain imagined paradise, an alchemic agent of change, whereas a British subject or someone from the Commonwealth may normally have a less dreamy view and a more cynical approach, as a post-colonial power that thinks it knows all the defects of the people it ruled.

Not gurus but fakirs, as they would say.

They think they see right through the charlatanism and get to the nitty gritty. Quite a divergence of views.

Europeans go through different phases of discovery in India. There's the imaginary India of the first phase, the India you have in your mind, that writers like Herman Hesse, Rabrindanath Tagore or Rudyard Kipling have etched in your imagination along with some other books, movies or even cartoons; the India 'that will change you', that will make you see a new face of humanity, harsher at times, enlightening at others.

It's the India of the Unicef and the Unesco, Yoga India, Ayurvedic India. And separate realities are immediately tailored in such islands of unreal India to cater to those needs. This imagined India is a business after all.

You can find her in Rishikesh, in Goa, in Kovalam, in Kochi, in Jaipur, it's coming to Tiruvannamalai, it's creeping in the backwaters of Kerala—Amazing India! Incredible India! A gigantic ashram for *Eat, Pray, Love* goras kind of India!

You pay for it, we produce it.

*

Some Europeans believe India is an experience that shortens your life, with its dengue, malaria, exotic diseases, crushing and unforgiving weather, and yet it is an experience that gives meaning to such allegedly shortened lives.

For many, it is worth it.

We often don't know why we love it. It goes against so many things Westerners have fought to gain and are proud of. Its dirt, poverty and unhygienic standards, still found in so many rural and urbanized contexts, are repelling at first.

India can be a liar and a thief. It stinks. It is corrupt. Or indifferent and merciless. Yet so many goras who are touched by it can't live without it and they suffer longingly when they are away for too long, just as in any instinctive, inexplicable and selfless love relationship. They call it home.

This is certainly the impact felt by vellais and goras who fall in love with India. It is in studying the dynamics of the pathology of the enamoured that we can explain the dazed behaviour of so many whiteys in India.

They will hear no reason, they fear nothing, they are ready for anything. They are ready to hug the whole world.

My experience has been that it is true—India does teach you its philosophy through the harshness it puts you through.

You may eventually learn non-attachment, if you want to survive the spectacle of misery, class and caste differences, traffic, bureaucracy, upset stomachs and frustration of a somewhat inexplicably stubborn mentality often expressed by government officers, be they the police or bureaucrats.

The idea that my own life is actually the same as that of a flower, like the yellow rose on my desk, the concept which says that a tree, or the thousands of other shapes of existence, including the inanimate, the rock, the car, the computer on which I'm typing this, the hypothesis that all of this is just one entity...well, this feeling can be truly perceived as permeating the culture.

You can breathe it in. You may be affected by it. Just by being here, you could experience this great, life-changing lesson. If you are open to it. If you know how to live it.

It's not something you need to learn in school, or by taking a Vedic philosophy class, nor something attained through reason and logic. It is something that is massaged into you by daily life, like an Ayurvedic oil. Soon it will reach your nervous system, it will calm you down, it will unconsciously make your head bob sideways using your third eye as a pivot. You will be forced to become patient. Or go mad.

It is true that in India you think different thoughts and feel different emotions. That is why so many whiteys are happily stuck here, even though they know that their life might be shorter here because they didn't grow up here with the anti-bodies (physical and mental) necessary to face all the harshness, without some price to be paid.

They (we) learn non-attachment. Even those who don't go native, don't learn the mantras, don't study the texts, don't contemplate changing their names to Harsh Sadhaka, as I had to do.

It may be a bit more difficult for those who hole up in gated communities housing expats. But it works marvels on the ones who open their arms to India, so that Mamma India may embrace them back.

Those may learn to accept death, which is always such a traumatizing drama in the West, as if we didn't know that everyone has an expiry date invisibly tattooed on them, like in a milk carton.

Death in the West is often an occasion to pull your hair out, torture your eyes and soul. Drama.

'Why? Why? Why did he or she have to die!' we scream in horror.

Erm…because it says so when you're born, maybe?

Yet centuries of Western science and penicillin still have not nurtured any higher capacity to accept what is 100 per cent guaranteed, along with taxes and the silence of mafia boss Gaetano Badalamenti: death.

India can provide this acceptance. India is a more developed country in this respect, while the so-called

West remains under-developed. That's because here, somehow, you get used to it. You learn to accept. You see it more often, you live with it, you carry on.

This is the India I unconsciously was looking for when I first travelled here in 2008.

I was one of those *yoga people*, as my best Indian friend Dirty Harri (Krishnan) calls us. I was in a moment of transition in life, a painful one.

And I was scared to come here. Terrified.

That is why, in 2008, I had bought a pocket water purifier in a specialty store in London before boarding a plane flying to Bangalore which would take me to do sun salutations and down-dogs and much more strenuous asanas at dawn in Mysore, under the charismatic gaze of the guru of Ashtanga yoga, Sri Patthabi Jois.

Yoga-people always go through a Mamma India phase, which is very spiritual, where you buy your dhoti or lungi near the temples you visit, you try your first kurtas and you learn the proper eating technique with three fingers of the right hand, trying not to gain too much weight with chapati, chutneys or masala dosas.

Then there's the Real India that sets in after you start living here, you try to open a bank account, buy a car, get a PAN (Permanent Account Number) Card, an Overseas Citizen of India Lifelong Residency Visa or a biometric data AADHAR identity card, you get five tickets for speeding, learn how to drive, how to race other drivers, how not to get mad, how not to get caught with your booze in the car at checkpoints in Tamil Nadu after visiting the bootlegger in Pondicherry, trying not to get sick to the stomach, avoiding dengue, whenever possible.

Yes, that India.

The India of kiss mobs vs moral brigades. Where people prefer AC full blast and double windows in their villas by the sea, instead of breathing in the sea breeze. The India of the 'Looking away syndrome'—the cohabitation of strong economic and social differences, where you discover there aren't four or five castes, but hundreds.

It's the phase in which you start thinking that Aldous Huxley was right when he stated that: 'To travel is to discover that everyone is wrong about other countries.'

It's also the India of privilege, that you can discover if you live here long enough as a foreigner, in this vibrantly growing, promising super-power.

It's the India I inhabit as a son-in-law of an Indian family.

The India I first discovered in the milestone year of 2008.

Embracing Mamma India in the watershed year of 2008

The Tangible, Smellable, Real Country vs the Imaginary Bharat

The year I first landed in India went down in meteorological text books as one of the most disastrous cyclone seasons in Indian modern history, killing 140 thousand people and causing 14 billion dollars in damages.

Getting accustomed to natural disasters wiping away thousands of lives is something I would eventually develop during my first 10 years in India. 'What to do?' Right?

Deaths have gone down, as prevention and warning systems have progressed during this decade, but you still get the seasonal murdering floods, landslides, and cyclones wiping away hundreds of families.

A World Bank economist once told me he picked Lithuania, Estonia and Latvia as his area of responsibility because he was determined to see lasting improvements within his lifetime: 'Most of my colleagues prefer tropical countries where people live in their underwear and where you work for years to build an economy, infrastructures and jobs. Then, a hurricane, a typhoon or a cyclone wipes it all away, and you start over. I mean, there's always endless work for the World Bank there, but not much progress within a lifetime.'

Some consider the World Bank as an extra natural disaster that occurs in these countries. That discussion is for another type of book.

The year of 2008 is not only commemorated as one of the worst cyclone seasons in history. It is also remembered for starting off as a most impressive year for the Indian economy while ending up as one best forgotten or, to say the least, to be archived as disastrous.

A watershed year, the year New India became what I call the 'Not-So-New India'.

Some might remember it as the era of Tata's Nano car (it was the rage back then), or the historic beginning of the Indian Premier League every cricket fan now raves about.

If you are a *literatus* or a *literata*, it was the year an Indian novelist, Aravind Adiga, won the Booker Prize for his debut novel *The White Tiger*.

Better pocket your positive thinking right here.

Sure, the year started in a most promising way. Sure, the economy was flying above 8 per cent and the sensex financial index was soaring over 21 thousand points. Double digit inflation was the only worry, then, as the head of government—that kind, white-bearded and turbaned man called Manmohan Singh—had just announced a 60,000 crore rupees debt relief package for farmers, which became the highlight of the annual budget.

The opposition members of parliament (MPs) were busy whipping out wads of cash in parliament, claiming money was being used to buy support for the ruling party—Congress. They didn't get much mileage from it.

Narendra Modi had not yet surfaced as their driving force. But the 2G telecom scam was beginning to put some cracks in the system. Not everyone had a smartphone, social media was looked at merely as a place to hook up.

Then the bubble popped, as the subprime crisis took its toll and stock markets crashed all over the world. Foreign investors pulled out billions of dollars from India. The sensex lost 60 per cent and dipped below 8 thousand points: one of the worst performers in the Asian markets. The fall of Lehman Brothers and the financial earthquake that hit banks worldwide did the rest. And, in India, growth estimates had to be revised downward as the world set off on a road to recession.

AC/DC's 'Highway to Hell' would be an appropriate soundtrack at this point.

Withdrawing a helping hand, American President Barack Obama announced taxes on US firms that outsourced. It was the beginning of the crisis for Indian call centers, which retrospectively turned out to be polishing schools for the poor in that upwardly mobile 'India that was'.

It was just an economic prelude to something worse

waiting to happen, as bombs were going off in Bangalore, Ahmedabad, New Delhi and Guwahati, blamed on Islamic fundamentalists.

It was only a build-up to the most daring terror strike in the history of independent India, which came about as I was leaving an Ayurvedic clinic in Trivandrum, where I had gone to explore the painfully purifying mysteries of the greasy Big Enema, of all things!

Ten gunmen armed with AK-47s, disembarked secretly in Mumbai and proceeded to attack iconic landmarks like the Taj Mahal Hotel, Chhatrapati Shivaji Terminus railway station and the Oberoi Trident Hotel. After days of battles, 179 people were dead and India had entered its new era.

Time to play AC/DC's 'Hell's Bells' now.

The lone survivor of the terrorist squad said he had arrived from Pakistan. Tension between India and the neighbouring nuclear power immediately hit the red alert. Military exercises at the border increased to war-talk level. This was 2008, a year that changed India and marked what India is still today, 10 years later.

These are the events that happened shortly before I walked into an enchanting open-air theatre on Chennai's Elliot's Beach to meet the woman who would later become my wife and change the course of my life. For the better. The woman who brought me to live in a house on the Bay of Bengal.

Arlanymor days

Of snakes, rats, frogs and other fauna teaching a
lesson about nature

It's early in the morning at the beach house where I now live with my wife, who's still sleeping upstairs. I'm standing by the kitchen sink, twisting open the Bialetti coffee machine—one of those moments when you're following an automatic routine while disregarding a threatening detail which might actually kill you.

My gaze is lost on a building site 300 metres away, partially barricading my view of the sun slowly soaring from the waters. Every time I stare at the new house intruding into our cherished isolation, I think we now have material proof that Osama bin Laden is alive, has resuscitated from the Indian Ocean, swam around Sri Lanka, reached the Bay of Bengal and crawled on our beach, where he began to build an exact replica of the Pakistani house where he allegedly had been shot dead.

I am sizing up the scaffolding around the construction of our local Abbottabad, when the corner of my eye glimpses something moving right next to my hand. And I instinctively reach for the Japanese cutting knife when…

Snake!

It immediately becomes clear we are both scared shitless. For a split second, we're both petrified. He, the reptile, trying to conceal his sinewy self behind three wooden cutting boards leaning against the wall; and I, the human, suddenly jumping back a metre and a half in a single leap.

'Snaaaaake!' I yell and run to find a stick to handle it with.

Growing up in Italy, I'd always thought snakes looked like cold, wet, and slimy-gross creatures. But after baby-sitting three rowdy boys, as a penniless high-school exchange student in Pensacola, Florida, I changed my mind.

At first, when I walked into the three imps' home, constellated with different glass boxes housing several types of snakes, I obviously thought I had been knowingly trapped in a nightmare. That's why no one else would baby-sit them, of course. 'Let's call that foreign student, he doesn't know any better,' was probably the rationale behind my part-time job.

It turned out I'd walked into one of those 'conquering your fears' turning points in life. I faced my ancestral terror and accepted to handle one of those creatures, which was actually warm and dry, quite pleasant to touch, really.

I mean, those Floridian critters were nothing close to the hypnotic gaze of the King cobras I'd recently shown my own son at Crocodile Bank, an hour up the road from the beach house in India.

These sacred animals have a particular magnetism,

shrouded in religious meaning here, a snake charm that can be galvanizing and hypnotic, once you get over the fear for your life.

It is in this respectful spirit that I now summon my inner Irula, the snake-capturing tribe of Tamil Nadu, and I face my demons in the shape of a terrified one metre long tree-snake who can't find his way out.

Action: Yank out the intruder with a long stick, then swipe him across the open space kitchen into the light-filled dining room area. He lands on the floor, a smooth and shiny cement base that makes it difficult for the limbless reptile to twist and turn on his way out.

So I pick him up again, swing him into the veranda, where I scoop him up and send him on a final launch across the green lawn into the unknown territory of a weed-covered yard.

There are two versions of what a tree snake can do to you.

My friend Shekar Dattatri, one of India's leading wildlife and conservation filmmakers, told me they are not poisonous and rather harmless.

Locals in the village of Paramankeni say that it's called a tree-snake because once it sinks its little teeth into your flesh, injecting its poison, it will then climb up a tree to watch your soul leave your body, as you lay dying.

I've later observed the same tree-snake swerve around the lawn while chasing a little tree-frog, hopelessly jumping into the bushes. I saw the *Dendrelaphis tristis* clutch the *Polypedates maculatus* in its jaws and swallow the little frog whole.

This is the tale I recount to prospective guests, just so they are prepared, the lesson that living in close contact with such strong nature can teach you. This is what I repeat to the guests who finally get over my cautionary tales and make it here.

In the city, you nurse your pathological arachnophobia, ophiophobia, entomophobia or musophobia, and off to phobia-land we go. These are ancient fears ingrained in millennia of survival reactions, keeping us, thinking monkeys, away from poisonous deaths.

After all, roughly 46 thousand people still die of snakebites in India every year, nearly half of the 100 thousand annual snakebite deaths in the whole world.

Yes, scary.

Yet, coming to a house in the middle of the casuarina and palm forests on the Coromandel Coast will force you to either put up or ship out.

Those who stay, see that after the first few hours or first night of anxiety, they relax and they co-habit. Until the next surprise.

Like finding that the detergent drawer of the washing machine has a tenant, when I yank it open to pour some fabric softener and I notice a tail slowly disappearing inside the machine.

A snake? A gecko? It couldn't have been one of the eight toads squatting between the crystals' cupboard and the kitchen wall. No tail on their little green bums.

Whenever I walk into the house after spending a few days away, I start dilating my nostrils, sniffing the air like a hunting dog, trying to catch a whiff of the worst type of intruders, which are actually more damaging than snakes.

It's gotta be that. I know it's gotta be. And I hate it.

I hate to have to bring out the cruel hunter, again.

I have tried to lead them out with my clarinet, like the Hamelin Pied Piper. They've made it clear they do not dance to my music.

Mice.

Co-habitation with mice or rats is not really possible if you like your bananas, your wooden furniture, your rice and all the other possible objects, like computers or phone cables, which these rodents enjoy stupidly sinking their teeth into.

Sometimes they enjoy tasting your wife's index finger while she sleeps, giving it a little chomp, just to see if she could be comestible. Apparently women tend to get bitten more often then men.

Or you may feel rat paws dancing on your hip and wander how the animal made it through the closed door and the tightly tucked mosquito net.

I know some temples in India worship mice, who are

represented by the mighty mouse Kubera, the greedy 'vehicle' of Lord Ganesh. Kubera is a reminder of the rodent-like obsession for desire gnawing away inside most humans.

I bow to the Sacred Mouse and the fine concept it represents, but I have not managed to find a way to domesticate them, so…I hope my acquired vegetarian Jain cousins, aunts and uncles forgive me, I am a heathen barbarian from a mostly carnivorous land, and even though I've had a pious 10 years streak as a vegetarian, I caved into the murderous plan to eradicate mice infestation in several attempts.

I did try the extended Jain family's wooden mouse box—the humanitarian option. The soft approach. The holy way.

'Just place a slightly roasted shred of coconut in the metal hook, or a banana,' my mother-in-law advised. 'The mouse will bite, find himself locked inside the box which you will then drive a few miles away and set the intruder free.' *Run Mickey Mouse, run!*

Never happened. Never took the bait once.

So, I descended into the criminal eco-damaging hell of rat poison.

This did not exonerate me from having to send to the creator a few of those rodents with more primordial methods, armed with a sponge-coated miniature baseball bat, a mop, a Himalayan walking stick, or any object that could crush the poor animal's neck.

You might've have guessed it by now: the little tail disappearing into the washing machine belongs to a cute little country mouse who has gnawed at some isolating material and made a comfy little two-bedroom apartment inside the LG detergent drawer.

He's still inside it as I write this, since I've not been able to dislodge him with boiling water, nor banging the stick on the machine, nor giving the machine a full cycle washing sweaty shirts and dirty towels.

That little mouse is a reminder of the challenges of living here at the beach. Of the challenges of living in India, intertwined as it is with such febrile nature.

'There's no paradise without mosquitos,' the saying goes. I'd add, 'nor without *Muscardinidae* mice'.

Cave canem by the sea

You've had the snakes. You had the mice. But I promised 18 stray dogs. And dogs you'll have.

It all starts with a black Pye-dog puppy. She was found as a newly born along with her brother Salvatore in the master bedroom's bathroom on the ground floor during construction.

She was born with this house.

Would it be too sentimental and irrational to say that Bagheera's persona is what gives this house its soul?

It would.

Bagheera is a now legendary black, wolfish, short-haired dog with intense intelligent eyes, and the soft movements of a grand dame with a past.

All dogs in a 20 km radius used to come and seek her when she went into heat. The nights used to be interrupted by visiting packs of dogs, howling into the night and regularly getting involved in brawls and in mating battles, a scene reflecting the stature Bagheera deserved in the canine community of Paramankeni and surrounding hamlets.

Salvatore would uselessly attempt to keep his sister in the exclusivity of an incestuous relationship. But he was no warrior.

One night we were forced to witness the two of them getting their genitals stuck into each other on the lawn, gazing at us as if saying:

'What the heck did we get ourselves into?'

'Ouch, that hurts, don't move that way!'

'No, you don't move that other way!'

What a horrible metaphor for relationships gone wrong.

We let the siblings figure it out by themselves, turning our embarrassed chins slightly to the side.

Salvatore is now long gone. He died of canine parvovirus, it seems. I found that name for him because of the way he begged for food, the expression he made when he looked at you wanting a caress, but afraid of being hit, probably having experienced the fishing village's rough terms of endearment. He reminded me of a neo-melodic Neapolitan singer ululating about love and loss. Salvatore rhymes with *amore*, yes.

I learned to be careful with names.

The little white puppy I named Giorgio Armani, because of the white hair reminiscent of his Italian fashion designer namesake, suddenly vanished into the night as he was going around the house. We heard a yelp and bye-bye Giorgio. Big forest cat must've gotten him.

Then there was Kate Moss.

Another unfortunate choice. She died as skinny as the British model who inspired her naming, possibly bitten by a snake, or taken by a wave of distemper or parvo.

No more fashion names.

We switched to literature. Safer bet, we thought.

One of Bagheera's grandchildren popped out with a very Prussian-looking, turned up moustache. So we named him Gunther, as in the German poet Gunther Grass. The vet later showed us it was actually a girl. So we called her 'A girl named Gunther' for a while, then switched to Guntherina, until distemper took her away too, after she inadvertently bit my calf causing me to get some scary anti-rabies shots.

We were luckier with another gender-free name dog. When it arrived, Ammu told us: 'Here's Jennifer,' which is how the villagers had called the dog. It soon became clear that Jennifer had a pair of canine testicles that inspired Ammu to rename him with the rather pedestrian 'Buggy', although I prefer to call him Bulgakov, because of the novel *Heart of a Dog*.

When he's sitting in a particularly elegant pose, crossing his wrists over the edge of the marble steps, I still call him Jennifer, to remind him of his feminine side. And then there's the nervous Zelda, as in Fitzgerald, runt of the litter saved from Chennai streets. Bulgakov and Zelda are both doing just fine, so far.

The two of them and Bagheera are now the wolfish pack guarding the house. My poet wife waxes fantastic on them, saying things like 'When they croon at the moon, they can sometimes sound like an a cappella band presiding over a pig-killing'. They are trying to sound like Celine Dion as they howl, beckoning us to go for the afternoon walk. Their moment of Dionspiration, she says.

Buggy is the only one who'll allow us to pet him. He's ever eager to be cuddled and massaged. Bagheera and Zelda have a don't-touch-me policy. We bond by howling together at the end of our walks, werewolves and hounds.

Bagheera is still the Queen of Paramankeni Beach— the longest surviving dog around here. She even pulled through a Greek-tragedy of a poisoning.

Back when our beach dog motel had reached the

untenable occupancy of 18 occupants, and visiting friends would look at us lowering their voices, saying things like 'You know you have a problem, here, right?' A farmer in the nearby village realized Bagheera had been plucking their chickens. We found the fifth decapitated chicken on our freshly sprinkled grass lawn.

And eye for an eye, a chicken for a chicken, must've been the aviculturist's rationale, as the farmer tossed a few poisoned rice balls at the gate of the property. Three puppies and two of Bagheera's daughters—Flopsy and Daisy—took the bait and died within the following 24 hours. Ammu buried them.

Bagheera survived that and countless beach assaults. The soul of this house is a survivor's soul.

*

The Narcissus vs Goldmund conundrum—should I stay or should I go?

As a teenager, one of my favourite novels was Herman Hesse's *Narcissus and Goldmund*, the tale of the amicable juxtaposition between Narcissus, an ascetic yet loveless scholar who never leaves the monastery and indulges in self-discovery strictly through study and meditation, and Goldmund, a young novice who, while collecting herbs in the forest, discovers carnal love with a woman and follows her to the village only to find out she's married.

She rejects him, but now he's tasted life outside the walls and continues an existence of travels and adventures throughout the world.

Although, as a young man, I did see the deep wisdom of Narcissus, I thought it would make sense to first try the path of experiential discovery set by Goldmund.

Stefania, a reader of my novels who lives in my hometown Valdagno in Italy, once wrote to me on Facebook this simple Narcissus-like question: 'How could you possibly have left our town? How can you live anywhere else but here?'

It is a pleasing valley, where I hail from. But, in 1982, Italy was still exiting the so-called 'years of lead'. Mafia, terrorism, corruption, plus a lot of killings and what looked like a hopeless future. Of course, things immediately began to get better as soon as I emigrated, as a teenage student looking for America in Northern Florida.

Yet, I never moved back to the province with the highest percentage of rain, nuns, priests, suicides, alcoholism and lap-dance bars. Yes, there must be a connection between this data. One day I will prove it.

So why move? Even as I migrated by myself at 16, I was told by the local Narcissuses about the weathered truism that 'you can't run away from yourself!'

Bullocks. We are not a monad, a single identity expressing itself invariably no matter where we are, no matter which language we speak.

'Our destiny is set by our character,' as Heraclitus reminds us in one of his philosophical fragments. But we can do something about it. Place and language do count. And they affect character.

All my life I've tried to leave Italy, and succeeded, but then returned to it. And now I'm trying to leave the only real homeland, language, Italian in my case, by writing here in my second language, English, which I've spoken since I turned 16.

All my life I tried to get out of Italy, now I am getting out of Italian. *Arrivederciiii!*

*

Does moving to a beach house in the tropics affect the personality of a Venetian who grew up half an hour ride from the ski slopes reading Herman Hesse before moving to America? You betcha.

For better or for worse? You'll be the judge of that, in these pages.

Does climate, cultural mood, customs and *mores* transform a human being? It depends a lot on how much you are willing to let yourself be transformed.

People who grew up in cultures which have solidified in eras of colonialism might develop a built-in mechanism preventing them from being greatly affected. They'll replicate their tightly cropped Commonwealth lawns in Australia, South Africa, India, America.

They'll recreate home, they'll mould the landscape to fit their nostalgia, sometimes even nostalgia of a place they've never seen. And nostalgia, as Nietzsche said, is the blank check issued to a weak mind.

Is that good? Bad? Not my problem to decide that. I'll leave it to you. I just know that because of the way my character was forged, I enjoy change.

I've loved observing my Americanization in my teens and twenties, and I don't mind that slight American accent you can capture in that esperanto inflexion of mine.

I've loved observing, in my thirties, my Mexicanization, my Argentinization, my Chileanization, while living in Latin America, and I've observed how the difficulties experienced living for one year in Madrid has made me somewhat impermeable to any Spanishization.

Yet, some may argue, I never evolved from that mountain boy from Valdagno, with those rough, sarcastic edges and a provincial, hopeful outlook in life, no matter the six formative and cosmopolitan years spent in New York City, the one year in a very international Washington D.C. University campus and becoming an Ivy Leaguer.

Place matters. So what does an isolated fisherman village do to a cosmopolitan soul? We'll discover it together.

Once in a house by the Bay of Bengal...

I had first seen the house that is now my Indian home in a very grainy video shot on a phone that my wife-to-be, Tishani, had emailed me.

It had not been finished. There were no windows. I couldn't really understand much from the grainy and shaky images she sent, just a lot of cement, some terraces, two floors, the sea nearby.

The foundations had been hit by a tsunami, putting a halt to construction. After dismissing an inspired German architect from Auroville who wanted to build some sort of futuristic bunker, my wife's family opted for a more classical architect who managed to put together beautifully, local elements along with classical ones in a neat villa with soft salmon colours and light gray columns, a tiled roof and slate-tiled verandas and terraces. It immediately made me think of a Cuban villa, reminiscent of the columns of Palladio—the architect from my home-province Vicenza.

Like all homes in the world, it requires a watchful gaze and regular interventions. Water pump, electricity, fans, erosion from the sea—it has its challenges, but it holds up marvellously considering the Northern and then Southern winds, bringing iodine, but also a corrosive saline mix and burning heat.

The house is coated with a secret formula paint that my chemical engineer father-in-law invented many years ago and is in high demand everywhere for its capacity to withstand the weather, shedding a micron of pellicle at every strong monsoon, and making the building look like it's been freshly painted after seven years of not touching it. The Abbottabad neighbours must have regretted not having used it, as they're often forced to repaint the entire building.

It is a barefoot, isolated life here, yes. Sometimes too much. Our rule is this: it's ok to talk to the dogs, but when you start hearing them talk back to you, it is time to go back to Chennai, at least for a couple of days and talk to humans.

The first time I went jogging by myself here, I heard a strange panting sound behind me.

As I turned, I saw three wild dogs silently running behind me, tongue out, literally at my heels. I learnt to deal with these packs of dogs, as we now lead Bagheera, Buggy-Bulgakov and Zelda on our afternoon walks.

It is a moment of wilderness, in which I have to bark, yell, throw coconut shells or driftwood at the attacking packs. The crazy white man.

Our three dogs and I walk away inebriated by a wolfish pride, wailing madly into the sea-breeze, having defended our turf, our Bagheera beach, from the ever continuous flow of dogs from the mainland.

They are not treated generously, these Indian Pariah dogs, or Pye-dogs for short. A few years ago, they found

400 of them in a mass grave in a fishing village towards Pondicherry.

They were all blue. Poisoned with cyanide which was leaking into the very same ocean where the fishermen were throwing their nets.

I mean, how uninformed can you be?

Forget about being inhuman or being illogical at tackling the serious issue of rabies and fear of dogs attacking villagers.

But poisoning your own waters by mistake?

We often walk by the fishermen on our strolls. Sometimes a lonely old, mute fishermen will leave the mending of his nets and walk up to me, putting a hand on his stomach, moving it to his mouth.

He wants money. I pull out the empty pockets of my jogging shorts. I've only got this expensive smartphone with me. Sorry, man.

By the way, Antonio, that's certainly one thing that the old fisherman thinks when he sees me: 'Gimme some rupees.'

Sometimes, in February, as fishermen gather on the shore to throw their nets in the shallow waters, there'll be a chant, or a hello, or a 'Come help us pull!' But, mostly, there's a healthy ignoring of each other—two worlds crossing that are too far away.

At first, I was tempted to be that anthropologically inclined journalist, that frustrated ethnographer from

Europe who comes and visits the village to find out how people live. My wife quickly gave me a good lesson on how to become Indian in that respect.

'If you go and visit them in their homes,' she told me a few years ago, 'you should expect them to come visit you here. Are you sure you want that? Or do you prefer to have your privacy and your freedom to be left alone and write without interruption?'

She had a point. It's, in its own way, a much more egalitarian stance than the alleged egalitarian push I thought I was feeling about 'levelling with the locals'.

That is the thing that us yoga people feel compelled to do. But, in its own way, it may be the most discriminatory thing to do within this context.

So, when I head out on our usual stroll with a friend visiting from the posh Notting Hill in London, and I see her wide, man-of-the-people, somewhat guilty-conscience smile to the fishermen, who are going about their regular business at the beach (the scant Muslim line-fishermen, the local lungi clad farmers, shepherds or loafers), I recognize my previous attitude.

It is that smile that creates the distance. It is that smile, that Western smile imitating the Indian smile, which is out of place.

I don't see any Indian friends smiling broadly at the locals. Smiling at the locals like that is a foreigners' prerogative.

And I am now a mappillai, so I'll just zip up that smile and won't go visit the locals for quite a while, unless there's some business to be discussed, which will inevitably be the case, as you'll find out later.

*

Mindful of the rock-climbing years of my youth, I sometimes hoist myself up to the top of the roof, here in Arlanymor, and I sit under the water tank on cement steps painted a pale orange hue.

I have, up there, a wide angle lens view of the Bay of Bengal, reaching down all the way to Pondicherry on my right, and inching up to Kalpakkam and Mahabalipuram, somewhere northwest.

You could almost touch Paramankeni village. The One World Academy Ashram is a stone's throw away. Motorbikes roaring on the ECR behind me, beyond the last stretch of the Buckingham canal where colourful turbaned ladies harvest mussels with their feet, immersed up to their necks, beyond the paddy fields.

The feeling of this wide expanse is quite different from what my young heart experienced in the verticality of the Dolomites, the Rockies or the Andes.

Down on the shore there's a frontier between two worlds, land and water. And, as in any frontier, a long strip of wet sand gathers the debris of both worlds.

The rotting olive ridley turtles, jelly fish, puffer fish,

cuttle fish, and the occasional dead sea-snakes feeding the crows, crabs and mussels, all mixed with the totems of society—the medicine bottles, the cheap rum, the toothbrushes, the miraculously intact giant lightbulbs used for night fishing, the lost chappal (flip flops), the shard of glass...

Corpses of technology and of nature rolling up and down the shore in their macabre dance, massaged into disintegration by the persevering waves. Organic matter and plastic matter slowly reverting to its constituent sand, dust, particles, molecules.

Looking out into the sea, imagining Myanmar, Thailand and Bangladesh, there, beyond the line at the end of my eyesight, it is different from imagining the future from the wall of a cliff. Rather, it is like imaging the most distant future—the line of death.

It is lingering there, a flat green tableau, hardly bothered by little fishing boats or some Indian Navy ship patrolling far far away. The sky is occasionally broken by a hunting osprey or black shoulder kite, or the smoky plume of a satellite being shot into space, the sparse airline flight, the very rare helicopter checking out the beach.

This frontier is not the one between the optimism of the mountain gaze, the barbarian palpitation for future conquests awaiting in the promising plain. Here, we are in front of the sometimes ominous hum-drum of the never ending tides, billows and white caps or white horses, as some frothy waves are sometimes called. There's something more final awaiting there. The unknown, out there, in the distant sea.

At night, since we're so far away from cities, the piercing stars bathing in dark blue cover everything and take over the show.

In the warm wind breezing through the coconut palms, all you can do is look up, play in your mind the know-it-all game of finding the Cassiopeia 'W' shaped constellation or seeing Orion the hunter actually bend the knee like Elvis Presley on a wild dance, and search for the constellation of the Sagittarius, exercise your eyes to see the colour of the planets in the South Indian sky.

But, at dawn, as I look out into this bucolic scene, it is often inevitable to catch a farmer, a fisherman, a worker or the watchman from the ashram up the beach squatting placidly for their morning defecation.

Haven't they heard of Modi's Swachh Bharat Abhiyan? The crazed vellai inside me would like to learn enough Tamil to just scream this question to them, but then I reconsider.

I decide to think about it more. There is something to be said in favour of the eco-friendly fertilization system of public defecation vs all that wasted toiled paper and the intricacies of the urban sewage system, the fact that in cities we live surrounded by faeces-packed pipes—below us, above us, in the faecal waltz in the walls around us. That's a bit disgusting too, but since we don't see it we're not aware of that simple fact.

Maybe now, as you read, you may be inside one of those rooms. And upon realizing this very simple architectural reality of our in-house sewage system you might reconsider the minor horror of finding a morning defecator on your walk.

Yet, I still hope I never run into one of their morning products, as I go jogging or walking barefoot on the beach in the morning, while I carefully study footprints leading back from the waves into the bushes, to spot that little hole that's been dug with the heels to create that transient water closet in the sand.

My friend Manu Joseph came on one such morning walk. He's a professional contrarian, great novelist, and the most original polemist-columnist in India. When I pointed out to him the morning twist dance of the beach defecator, he almost took it personally.

'Oh, no, they're not doing that,' he blurted, almost offended, 'rural Indians are not like dogs, covering their poop with their feet!'

'Well, look a little longer, Manu, that's exactly what's going on here. It's called nature. Look, they're digging the sand-bidet, don't you see?'

'Well, I do see that they have pretty plump buttocks in this part of Tamil Nadu...' Manu said, squinting, 'which means they are rather prosperous and that they eat well!'

As V.S. Naipaul has somewhat disdainfully written in *Area of Darkness*: 'Indians defecate everywhere. They defecate, mostly, beside the railway tracks. But they also defecate on the beaches; they defecate on the hills; they defecate on the river banks; they defecate on the streets; they never look for cover.'

I confess that in order to understand this important and embarrassing Indian phenomenon involving at least 600 million people without bathrooms, once, during a solitary morning stroll on the deserted beach, I gave it a try myself.

I wanted to see if there was something poetic in this process. I had observed the locals doing what is called the Asian squat, which I, of course, cannot master because of my Western buttocks—something about the gluteus Maximus' conformation, I've been told.

When I catch these men staring inspiredly into the horizon, looking at the ravishing Surya rising from the waters at dawn, I imagine them mixing a moan of colonic relief with a sigh of spiritual bliss.

I often see them go out in small groups. Public defecators love to share the experience. They wait, they chat, they gaze at the scenery, as they wait for nature to take its gravitational course.

Bombs away!

Purge them toxins!

Off they go, those brownish Led Zeppelins without helix nor rudder!

Most of the time I find them walking towards the Vaishale Prawn Hatchery of Mugaiyur, heading north. They squat merrily in front of the appropriately named 'Get Together' resort. Or I stumble upon them and their daily products by the even more appropriately named beach villa 'Extasea', as they seem to reach some sort of bowel ecstasy in front of the sea.

So one day I did go out there, determined to fully grasp the process by experiencing it, in the name of the best tradition of 'New Journalism'.

I felt like the Gay Talese of defecation, the George Plimpton of bowel movements, the Norman Mailer of public pooping!

I loosened my bathing suit, lowered it to my knees, lifted my t-shirt and clipped it between chin and sternum as I squatted down, looking around furtively.

I pushed, I waited. I pushed, and waited. I felt like a Gollum hoping to produce his 'Tresssure'.

Nope. I realized that probably some mental mechanism, some prudery, some learned behavioural constraint was keeping me particularly constipated at that moment. So I never had the pleasure to discover first hand what it must feel like to do it in the sea-water washed sand. No get-together *extasea* for me.

But it cannot be said I didn't try, for tried I have, alas failing.

*

The soundtrack of our lives here in Arlanymor is made up by your regular Hindu temple speakers in the distance, the occasional fireworks from the villages, and, during fishing season, the put-putting of dozens of small fishing boats, patrolling the ocean starting around 5 am.

In the beginning, it was magical, then simply annoying. Oh, well, a good time to head out through the little rusty gate for the beach morning stroll, come back and have muesli and orange juice, stuff that old Bialetti coffee machine with fresh Cariappa coffee from the Kodaikanal hills and start writing until lunch, which is often *schiaffoni* pasta with sauce made with tomatoes from our garden, fresh basil plucked from the pot.

The solitude that is created here is intense—the one I feel now as I write this, with my wife having returned to Chennai, with the caretaker Ammu having gone to Koovathur village to pay the electricity bill and see her friends.

All I hear now is the muffled sound of waves, which I can spy through the chik blinds and the shut windows.

The sea is growing rambunctious. It is 10:30 in the morning and life at the beach is still.

'This is a properly isolated place,' says William

Dalrymple, when he comes to stay a few days. And several other friends have been here, all in need of a few hours or days before getting adjusted to the lack of a WiFi connection, no TV, no traffic noise. Beppe, Ortensia, Fabrizio, Cristina, Taiye, Alessandro, Gary, Pankaj, Mary—I shuffle in my mind the many names and faces of friends who visited and ponder on how they reacted.

You can study their expressions in the photos we click on the marble stairways facing the entrance, the goodbye group shot we often subject our parting guests to. They seem mostly serene, having been able to slow down time, however short their stay.

They've gotten into this strange, out of the times groove, the transcendental isolation that it's so easy to make fun of or to envy in our famously interconnected world.

*

The most interesting man in the world syndrome

I did not arrive to my isolated life in Arlanymor unprepared. This is graduate school, or rather, a PhD in isolation. But I did go to undergraduate school.

At one point in my life I moved to a small cabin in the hills an hour and half north of Rome, in the hinterland of Civitavecchia. I was finishing my first novel and needed a place to stay. I was surrounded by forests, wild boars, and donkeys.

Allumiere had the unusual distinction of having its own Palio, just like Siena, a Medieval-era horse race around the city main square, pitting borough against borough. Only that here they use donkeys instead of horses!

Life in the little hut, one bedroom, one bathroom, a dining room with a fireplace, was bliss and hell.

I started a vegetable garden there too. I managed to extract eggplants and tomatoes from the land. I'd go running in the morning, cook myself meals, hear the croaking voice coming from my own throat, as I answered the phone after a few days without talking to anyone, as I was getting over a painful separation.

Two books emerged from that phase. A novel and a collection of short stories. It's a weird choice for gregarious Italians, it's weird for many Indians as well, unless you are shifting into sadhu mode, this choice to live in a very rural place, not being a naturalist or a hippie, but a writer.

Maybe it's because of all the stories and experiences accumulated with a peripatetic (some would say more pathetic than peri) full life. Maybe I needed to purge all that I've seen and heard, also in my job, as a journalist and foreign correspondent, that pushed me to witness first hand, a lot of misery and suffering in many parts of the world. It is a cleanse of sorts, perhaps, a way to let the reverberation of all those memories settle and vanish, re-awakening some new interest in the samsara of the human game.

It is not the most obvious choice, I realize it. It's... weird.

The first time I was called 'weird' was in high-school in America, where I was an exchange student at 16, a few miles from Pensacola in the Florida panhandle, closer to Alabama than to anything else.

'Weird.' Maybe it was my accent. My being a foreigner. Or something more. I liked it. I recognized it. I welcomed it. Whatever that means. Weird mappillai. Ok. I'll take it.

What does weird mean? Bizarre? Freaky?

You wouldn't believe it, but 'wyrd' is an ancient Germanic word which meant 'destiny', or 'having a supernatural power to control destiny'. Later, in the 19th century, it took on the meaning of 'unearthly', 'inhuman', and later it started to indicate what is strange and bizarre.

When I go back to Italy I have a brilliant situationist artist friend, Fulvio Abbate, who regularly interviews me for his online channel, Teledurruti. Mostly he uses me to sound off his frustrations.

'The most interesting and enviable man in the world!' he screams on videos he posts immediately after we exit the Trattoria da Lucia al Mattonato in Trastevere, one of the few authentic places left in that tourist-run Roman neighbourhood where my son still lives.

He depicts me as what it must look like from the outside, this Italian who made it out of that constant flow of complaints about a life with too many taxes, corrupt politicians, lack of meritocracy, difficulty in expressing artistic talent, in making a decent living without cheating or compromising ethically, at some point in your life.

It seems I have been suffering for decades from a not-so-rare disease commonly known as 'the most interesting man in the world syndrome'.

This is how my friend Miguel Syjuco has nicknamed me, tired of hearing just how many things I had done and in such diverse, exotic places. He was comparing my biography to a now famous viral TV advertisement— the parody of a leathery skinned, white stubbled world adventurer showing off his dazzling life. And stooping to drink a specific Mexican beer.

It's a syndrome largely affecting privileged and insecure white males who have been chasing the exotic most of their adult lives and can account for not much more that a sum of far flung experiences. This just when 'the exotic' has become out-of-fashion and too politically incorrect to even mention.

Just to give you an example, as I find myself at the dinner table in a writers' residency in Civitella Ranieri, a 15th century castle in the heart of Umbria...see what

I'm getting at? Even the beginning of this story is worthy of what is known as the M.I.M.I.T.W. syndrome.

The setting is idyllic. At night I find no trace of the ghost of the pregnant nun it is rumoured was walled alive in the castle centuries ago. As I look out of the window in the early morning mist, I hear the familiar, exhilarating, chirping sound of isolation. Maybe it's just the swallows.

But, later, when I find myself at the long dinner table, I chat with fellow resident writer Yvonne Adhiambo Owuor, an Afro-politan writer from Nairobi, so I can tell her about that afternoon in '95 when I was giving rides to masais in a borrowed jeep in Maasai Mara or when a mysterious British army truck emerged from the darkness during a storm near Lake Victoria, where I'd gotten stuck in the middle of my Kenyan night...

Chinese video-artist Liang Yue asks if I've visited her hometown Shanghai. Of course, I have. I was aboard the MV Greenpeace when we sailed illegally into Chinese waters and were boarded by the Coast Guard in the Shanghai harbour and threatened with 10 years in jail for counter-revolutionary activities, as the eco-militants were protesting nuclear testing still happening in the Lop Nor desert...

Then I meet Halldór Smárason, a composer from Iceland, so I can tell him about being busted by the cops during a loud party in the outskirts of Reykjavik when

I traveled there once, to interview a scientist conducting a mysterious genetic project for a documentary on successful ageing which I was producing…

Then Chris Paul Harman, a Canadian composer, just needs to know about my New Year's Eve in freezing, hyper-remote Winnipeg, Manitoba in '89, but also Eloisa Morra, the Italian writer from the unknown town of Tolfa, the hillbillies of Rome, will gawk at the revelation that in 2005 I actually lived right next door to her, in that wood log cabin in Allumiere, my Walden Pond.

By the way, did you know this very same Umbrian castle where we gather to write, compose or paint was owned by Ranieri Can, a Most Serene Republic of Venice warrior who defeated the Hungarian Count of Ozora. 'Oh yes, I know Ozora, in Hungary, of course, I've been there to a psy-rave party in 2011 when Raja Ram was playing the flute and spinning and…'

Ok, you get the unbearable picture. This is 'the most interesting man in the world syndrome'.

I have to incarnate that mythology, it is my dharma. Sorry.

But, now, in Arlanymor, the challenge of this phase of life is learning to stand still. In isolation. To learn to appreciate tranquility, after much nomadic stirring.

*

Finding your right 'loneliness to company' ratio

Back in 1993, I saw a movie called *Thirty-Two Short Films About Glenn Gould*. A phrase repeated by the actor, interpreting the pianist and composer Glenn Gould, stuck with me for decades.

It goes something like this in my memory, but don't quote me on this: 'People operate on a percentage system. They may need to be with other people 80 per cent of the time and by themselves 20 per cent of the time. Or it's the other way around. Everyone has a different percentage, a different ration. Understanding what your percentage is, can bring you some balance in life.'

He didn't really say it like this but that is the lesson I bring with me through the haze of partial amnesia, through the reconstruction of what I found useful in that distant phrase.

In the overcrowded societies of Europe or Asia, voluntary isolation is the most enviable luxury you could hope for.

In the splendid seclusion I've reached in Arlanymor, I sense I calmed down a long-running Kubera-like ambition. I still have my goals, the books I want to write, the Asia I'm trying to understand while writing about what happens here. Dharma, again? Perhaps. But it's all more measured. It could be age. It could be life in Arlanymor, where civilization seems to drift away, beyond the blue wooden gate.

Here I think in simpler terms, as Paul Gauguin used to say of his Asian exile. Old rancors have faded into nothing, where they belonged, simpler pleasures appear more brilliantly in my heart, like watching the egrets, the sun refracting on the sea's skin, contemplating the new shade of red of a flower.

I work on my books from dawn to lunch, and write my articles in the afternoons, interrupted by a one hour walk after tea time.

Tomorrow will be like today. There's no weekend.

Peace descends upon me, worries evaporate in the casuarina forest, never to return.

Until I have to open that gate again.

Because at some point it has to end. When the dogs start talking back to you, when their howling become messages. Go, go, gooooo.

That's when I get to drive back to a metropolitan area of 8 million people, many of whom have a very dubious concept of road rules.

So let's drive together, back to Chennai...

DRAVIDIAN DAYS

Getting five speeding tickets, mastering the 'Ganesh will save me' merging manoeuvre, understanding cities through their roads, negotiating bribes, and driving around with Hitler before running into Stalin and the Theosophical Society.

White man's privilege in Chennai's spiral traffic

Or practical lessons in Indian facial & hand gestures + driving techniques

It's time for that Italian manoeuvre to beat the traffic. Cross over, start a U-turn by rolling down the window, waving my arm wildly at incoming traffic and warn I'm going to go for it.

Then shove the nose of the car into the opposite lane, force an auto-rickshaw, a moped, a bike and a car to slam on their brakes and let me ease into their lane, shaving a millimetre off the bark of a nearby poplar tree.

'Amazing what a white arm can do in Chennai traffic, ay?' I comment to my wife and to my mother-in-law, who's nervously clutching the fake leather seat in the back.

'Oh, you think it's that post-colonial power still?' My wife asks.

'Guaranteed. Did you see anyone complain? No one. It's that crazy Westerner again. They're too shocked to start an argument. Not a beep, nor a peep. White man's privilege!'

Traffic in Chennai? Worst traffic in India.

I mean there's Auroville. That's right—try driving out or into Auroville at night and you'll see. You probably think peace and quiet, spirituality and brotherhood.

Forget it. Wild cattle roaming the dark, narrow and badly paved roads. Bicycles without a headlight in zero public lighting are more likely what you'll get.

Everyone's used to the skinny holy cows roaming about the highway on the East Coast Road as the engine hits 120 km/hr. And I'm no newcomer to bovine-dodging either.

But Auroville at night, I promise, will make you lose one point of your eyesight and maybe a square cm of hair somewhere in your receding hairline. Not to mention the washed up, weathered vellais: Italians, Germans, Belgians, French, Canadians, Americans who go Easy Rider, 'head out on the highway looking for adventure, for whatever comes our way...b-b-b-booooorn to be wiiiiiild!'

They haven't gotten the Indian flow yet, so they're accelerating and braking suddenly, all with the wrong rhythm—too jumpy and jerky for the context of such deep forest darkness.

They haven't understood yet the silent, feigning mediation, that cross between indifference to incoming traffic and survivalist alertness which is inbred in any living Indian driver, including Overseas Citizens of India residents, like myself.

They haven't mastered the 'Ganesh will save me' lane merging technique: the motorcycle driver who never looks to his right, as he merges into a lane, knowing that if a truck wipes him away, that is the will of the gods.

It's actually more subtle than that. It's a game of feigning indifference. A competition among non-attached folks in showing the other you don't care what happens. I don't care more than you don't care. See? I'm not even looking!

And it's even more complicated than that, really. It's a game about pretending you do not have peripheral vision and expecting the incoming driver to have it, so he is the one forced to step on the breaks before ramming into you.

Ram ram, jai jai ram. Ram ram on them brakes!

But there's a simple technique to avoid heart-attacks at every merging motorcyclist: just pretend to be even more unaware of the 'Ganesh will save me' motorcyclist. His peripheral vision will miraculously re-awaken. He will swerve at the right time, stay off the road and let you pass.

If Auroville is the worst for back street driving, Chennai is the king of road stomach acid.

I've marched my wheels on the asphalts of Delhi, Kolkata, Mumbai, Bangalore, Kochi, Kovalam, Trivandrum, Gangtok, Goa, Guwahati, Shillong, Shekawati and more.

Yet, Chennai wins and here's why.

In the symbiosis of man and automotive vehicle, traffic is just an extension of the urban culture's nervous system.

There is one sure way to understand a city—observe meticulously how people drive in it. And how they drive into each other.

How do Chennai spirals differ from Mumbai's snakes or Delhi's amphibian toads; the geometric/zoological gridlock metaphors for different shapes of car clusters?

Delhi has got imperial traffic and imperial gridlocks. It means you get stuck, mostly. In flooded lanes, in irrational choices at roundabouts or simply by overcrowding. You get frustrated if you're in a hurry to improve your career, gain power, meet influential people who will help your dharmatic quest for power.

Mumbai thinks it has traffic, but it has lane dividers! How serious can it be? You get stuck, sure. But it's a problem only if you have a Westernized obsession with results, appointments, delivering on time, and such devilish fixations. If you just turn on the radio and you have automatic gears, you should be fine, really.

Bangalore is a mess, three hours to get to the airport. Ok, but you let the Uber driver lose a year of his life by worrying and sounding his horn, while you check your Instagram in the back seat.

Again, it has to do with where you're going, not necessarily with how bad your experience is at the moment. Yes, lethal fumes, yeeesss overheating engines, I know, and, yes, constantly paying attention to see if someone cuts in front of you and then you find yourself in the same spot for an hour, while the lanes to your left and right are slowly flowing to their destiny.

Fine. Nothing that can't be cured with a little new age music as a soundtrack.

But Chennai...there's no way you can do that in the traffic nightmare capital of the country known for traffic nightmares. This city did not develop with a plan. It went from 40 thousand people to eight million in less than a century.

Very few traffic dividers, narrow two-lane roads designed for one bullock cart at a time, filled with six lane traffic, garnished by bee-hives of mopeds and bikes.

Here, the name of the game is 'chicken'. Not just to avoid cars that cut in front of you, but to avoid incoming traffic from jumping into your lane and really getting you, the jouster, stuck for a long, anarchic while. The vital question is: who will swerve first?

This is just a reminder of the precariousness of our position in society, of the fleeting nature of existence. Again, India teaches its Vedic lessons in everyday life, if you know how to interpret it.

Which is the whole point—non-attachment to your spot in the lane while you reincarnate into your next spot in line.

But it's a struggle because your dharma is to get somewhere. So you press on that pedal and you hop on forward, while your nemesis in incoming traffic does the same, shoved into your lane by a car cutting in from the side.

Rule number one is, if you haven't grown up here: learn the Indian wrist twist. Once you master that, you can do anything in traffic. You'll be respected. Even better, you'll be understood.

A few years ago, an Indian friend spent a considerable chunk of a dinner conversation trying to prove to me that only Indians, born and bred in India, can properly perform the Indian wrist twist. I beg to differ. I claim that even adopted Indians like me can get close to mastering it.

This gesture, generally known as the 'change-the-light-bulb move', has two different variables with diverse meaning: the vertical glide and the horizontal glide.

First: the vertical.

Simply put, you hold up your forearm in front of your face, palm out. As you twist the palm towards your face, you slowly spread your fingers as widely as you can, meanwhile you tilt your wrist as if you were carrying a tray full of idlis.

This is when you have to slightly bend your pinky finger and thrust into the void your arched thumb. Your hand will look like a blossomed lotus held in front of your face.

Very cosmic, I know.

But if you accompany it with a totally straight face

and a slightly fixated gaze into the eyes of the driver who's at the wheel in the car next to yours it will mean: 'What the f*@?k, bro? What do you think you're doing, man?!'

That's known as 'the vertical wrist twist'.

Then: the horizontal.

If you use the twist horizontally, by moving your hand from your armpit sliding slowly out and accompanying it with the notorious Indian head bob (keeping the third eye spot between your eyebrows as the pivot and swinging your chin left and right) this gesture can be used as a reply to the vertical wrist twist and it'll mean, in traffic: 'Com'n, dude, you are the one who cut in front of me!? Let me pass. That means, now!'

It all happens like that in Tamil Nadu, where aggression, like sexuality, is kept mostly where it belongs: repressed.

I got my first lesson in traffic behaviour in Chennai while having one of my Mediterranean moments. You know, when the blood heats up, you start identifying with the matriculation number of the piece of metal and rubber you're driving and you take it personally.

You will be the car that gets ahead! And so you race through an insane gobble of Maruti Suzukis, Ecosports, Dusters, any of those average, decent cars of Not So New India, machines that can take the dry season pot-holes as well as the monsoon flooding.

After a few close calls, the time comes when you and

your nemesis are both stuck at the traffic light. This is the moment when I, as a pitta passion-prone Southern European, feel like the time has come to roll down the window, start a series of insulting gestures with my hands meaning, in Italian *gesturese* or Gesturian language: 'Who do you think you are? Are you mad to drive like that? I am more man than you are and I will demonstrate it to you with impressive swiftness in automotive manoeuvres, as I have already done in the last 15 minutes.'

Then, I would normally shout something about the other driver's mother, his in-breeding parents, the limited faithfulness of his wife and other such not-so-well documented theories about the total stranger who, meanwhile, is giving me the Tamil treatment.

In fact, he is wearing the mandatory moustache, the out of fashion long hair covering his neck, the bald spot and the wrap-around dark shades, most likely signalling some sort of unverifiable proximity to either the powerful AIADMK or the DMK Dravidian political parties.

In the brilliance of his nicely pressed white shirt, a blinding huge smile opens up in his fully lipped mouth as he gives me the slow-motion Tamil version of the infamous Indian head bob, indicating: I'm more cool-headed than you are. I've gotten here without a drop of sweat. This is my turf. I belong. I'm gonna jump ahead of your car within the next three moves after the light turns green.'

What am I to do, but to simply smile back in the widest possible way and realize this is exactly what will happen and so I let it happen and thank Chennai traffic for this lesson, sit back, and follow the instructions glued to the back of the car of this well-humoured prankster/road-warrior whose bumper sticker invites me to 'Relaaax'.

So, yes, Chennai has the worst traffic in India.

And yet I know 80-year-old Malayalis who have lived here most of their lives and whose idea of a fun afternoon is to just go out for a drive. Yes, really.

Driving in Chennai is one sure cure to its main defect: it's a boring city, unless you work for organized crime and political parties, which is often the same thing as proven by countless trials and convictions through the decades. I mean, I'm sure it can be fun but I have a hard time finding out how.

You may think things get better as you leave the city. You may be deluded into believing that a highway with a panoramic nomenclature such as 'The East Coast Road' will regale you with the cruising pleasure you dream of in India; this stretch of asphalt that takes you from Chennai to Cuddalore via Pondicherry on what is technically State Highway 49, a two-lane and, at times, four-lane 'highway' in Tamil Nadu, built along the coast of the Bay of Bengal.

ECR.

East, the light of dawn.

Coast, like riding a Harley on Pacific Coast Highway in California.

Road, that feeling of familiarity and human dimension.

The ECR leads you first to Fishermen's cove, to Arun and Murthy's Surf Spot at Covelong's point, then to the touristic Mamallapuram, a little ancient temple on a promontory surrounded by the waters of the Bay of Bengal, the city of the Seven Pagodas and incredible carved rocks, and then it takes you to the ever utopian Auroville community, and the White Town (with the white buildings for the white people) in Pondicherry, now renamed Puducherry, and on to the suggestive Chidambaram with the invisible *shivalingam*, which might seem like a contradiction, but it's theologically the most honest concept: you adore something that you can't see. And on to the colonial Tranquebar, before getting lost into a quite different, southern Tamil Nadu, into the dreamy Chettinad of Victorian villas and stunning temples.

So you think that after you drive by the appropriately named Dizzy World amusement park, running into a few cars with signs that preemptively stop you from personal insults by telling you things like 'My Mother is Great' or 'Without Wife/No Life', you will finally reach the toll booth where you dish out your 35 rupees while yelling

'Single' even though you're married, and you think now comes the time to hit the gas.

But it ain't.

Nothing changes.

Same amount of cows, trucks, people crossing the road with loads of stuff on their head, under their arms, dragged in carts behind them or pushed in front of them and especially in front of your car, now roaring in mechanical frustration.

*

Driving up and down the ECR has inspired in me the idea of a survival video-game. 'ECR EXPRESS' gets its name from the most dangerous animal in the Tamil traffic kingdom: the green Ecr Express bus.

It's a mafia. It is known. These drivers know no limits. They have the right protection with the authorities, evidently.

What happens is simple, and the rule can be applied to all Indian traffic. It's an ancient canon called the Law of the Jungle: the biggest vehicle has the right of way.

The structure which will get the most damage has to yield. Moped gives way to motorbike, which gives way to Tata Nano, which makes way for Maruti Suzuki, shared autos—the insidious school van—giving way to Ecosport, giving way to foreign SUV giving way to bus or truck.

The big guy rules. No nobility of strength, but the clarity and reliability of bullying.

It's actually refreshing and leads to no confusion. You will be trampled upon. You are smaller, get out of the way.

So, in this video game, you start by riding a bicycle. As you survive after the first three km, you will be awarded a better vehicle, a moped and then a motorcycle, on an on, until you go up the gear-chain until you get to drive an ECR Express bus.

Ah, final success. You can bully everyone now.

The purpose of the game is to arrive at your destination alive and without causing too many casualties. The driver must dodge swiftly in-coming buses, cars, mopeds stacked with paraphernalia, avoid roadblocks from police patrols looking for smuggled alcohol, as it is illegal to cross state lines with booze.

You have to avoid running over holy men and sadhus, turbaned farmers, goats, elephants, tigers, cobras, buffaloes, students texting, drunk priests, falling cargo, furious bus conductors—all these constitute elements to be dodged and avoided during the maddening drive.

Night driving will be particularly dangerous because everyone constantly keeps their high-beams on and people leaving wedding parties will drive more recklessly.

Your eyes will look like you're getting the Ludwig treatment in *A Clockwork Orange*, lids stapled to your cheeks and eyebrows.

As your car crashes, it will have a chance to 'reincarnate' in a new avatar but at a lower level.

A VW Polo will become an auto-rickshaw, upon crashing will convert into a motorcycle, a moped, and back to bicycle and finally, if that crashes too, you will see only a wheel, slowly rolling all alone down the ECR, to the 'GAME OVER' part, while the Vedic subtitle appears: 'The wheel of life'.

Different drivers will have different protecting deities (Shiva, Vishnu, Ganesh, Hanuman, etc.) to which they can appeal for extra credits (gas, time, bigger wheels) through the appropriate mantras, which are also gained through points (summed thanks to safer driving).

As you rise through the levels of driving skills, starting with just two arms, you gain more arms. As you move toward greater 'enlightenment' having survived the high-beams, you have more arms at your disposal, for shifting, answering the phone, flicking high-beams and even giving alms at stoplights, while simultaneously edging that other driver out.

Of course, given the dangers of driving, you could conceivably lose one or more of your arms too. A less compassionate manoeuvre will cause a loss of an arm. Armless, you can't drive and you crash.

It actually could be played in schools as a fun alternative to driver's education.

But what is the point of driver's education when

any traffic infraction can be solved with a few hundred rupees?

Bribes are an integral part of life in many countries.

Once in the streets of Merida in the Yucatan Peninsula of Mexico, I was stopped by a traffic policeman who said he could either give me a ticket or I could give him some money for a soft drink since his job required him to stay out in the heat. '*Algo por un refrescooo?*' is the most common question a copper will formulate. 'Got something to give me so I can buy myself a drink?'

We then started negotiating in a most complex manner. He said we should apply Article 60, and I thought it would be more appropriate to apply Article 20. Both numbers referring to the amounts of pesos to be paid in order to let me go.

They call it *la mordita*, the nibble, the small bite—a lesser price to pay illegally in order to avoid paying a larger one legally.

I have been given a few speeding tickets already in India. This was while driving out of Chennai to reach the ECR.

I was going at 55 km/hr in a 40 km/hr speed limit zone in a long, straight, stretch of road where three over-fed cops were hiding in the shade with a tripod and a speed-reader.

I've learned not to contest the truth and to pay what is due. They were right, I was wrong. For, however little the infraction, there was a mistake on my part and the amount, by my standards, was more reasonable than the 200 euros I've had to pay in Italy for a similar mistake.

But once, the officer in charge ran after my car after I had already paid the ticket. He slightly tapped the side of the vehicle to ask me to stop.

I rolled down the window and he pointed to his portable tickets machine. He had not printed the receipt yet.

It felt like it was important for him to give me proof of a regular ticket. No foul play here.

But on another occasion, I was already into the city streets, back from surviving the ECR drive from the beach house and I made an extremely illegal turn, right into the arms of a traffic patrol stationed at the cross road.

I was waved down by a tall, muscular, regularly moustachioed Tamil officer with a crafty smile and low command of English. After getting my driver's license and asking me where I lived and where I worked, he went to the back of the car to confabulate with his superior.

Maybe because of white man's privilege, again, or because an Italian born in Switzerland with a US driver's licence, but teaching in a college in Chennai was already complicated enough, it seemed like the officer in charge of the patrol wanted to let me go without a ticket. There was obviously a discussion about it, though.

So when the cop gave me back my documents, he leaned his big forearms on my rolled down window. Looking straight at me with that sneaky, yet languid gaze he said: 'Any compliments?'

I realized he wanted a bribe, but I couldn't help blurting out: 'Sure man, you have the most beautiful moustache I've ever seen!'

As I rolled up the window, I was laughing so hard inside myself that I thought it wasn't fair. This man had provided me with an anecdote I would use for years. He deserved to be paid.

I reached into my pocket, rolled down the window and slipped him a 500-rupee bill, which he received with a totally indifferent expression.

And I took off.

*

As I plunge into the writing of this book, I find myself speeding again down the ECR south of Chennai, heading to the beach house to finish my manuscript. A tall Tamil police officer walks to the middle of the road and points to the side.

I slow down, put in park, roll down the window.

'You know you were going 88 km per hour?'

'No, I'm sorry, I didn't notice.'

'And you know this is a 60 km per hour driving zone?'

'No, I didn't know that either. There are no signs.'

'There are signs.'

'I must've missed them because of all the traffic and people cutting in front of me.'

'Or maybe because you were going too fast?'

I'm wearing my sunglasses, I'm smiling. He catches on I'm not nervous. I'm a vellai, but he must perceive, I think, that I am familiar with local customs.

'I have a machine here that says you were going 88 km per hour, I can show you.'

'No, no, I am not contesting that I was not driving 88 km per hour, I'm not saying you are wrong at all. It may very well be.'

And I shut up, smiling.

'Licence please.' I give it to him. It's my New York driver's licence.

'Oh, American...' he hints with a smile.

'Well, Italian and American, but not Italian-American exactly, but I'm Italian and also I guess a little bit American, in a way, I mean...'

He doesn't really seem interested in my identity crisis.

'International drivers' licence?'

I pull it out. So he calls over another guy, probably his superior, who walks over carrying a box with a screen indicating my speed violation.

'It'll be 500 rupees,' he says.

Round numbers are suspicious.

'Can I have a receipt?'

'Well,' he fumbles, 'you see, international is 500 rupees...'

I turn over my hand wallet so he catches a glimpse of my biometric ID—my precious Aadhaar card.

'Oh, you have an Aadhaar card, too?'

'Yes, I live here, I do have an Aadhaar.'

'Oh, ok, in that case it is less...'

I come to his rescue, showing him I only have 2000-rupee bills and very few hundreds.

'I'm sorry I don't have a 500, I only have 300.'

'Ok,' he says. 'Give me 300, no receipt, ok? It's 500 for foreigner, but you have Aadhaar card so 300...Ok?'

'Ah-huh...right...'

We both give each other the wide, slow Tamil-style teeth-flash of mutual understanding and I hand over gleefully a brand new yellow 200-rupee bill accompanied by a blue 100, feeling that, finally, I have truly earned my local driver badge.

I can now be asked for bribes at acceptable Tamil Nadu middle class, middle-aged man prices (although I might have overpaid by 100 rupees, I think.)

I step on the gas and take off reaching 100 km/hr again in a few seconds.

Bribing your way into the future

Dealing with the kind extortionists of our daily lives

There is something exciting in the air in this noisy, overcrowded and sweat-inducing Chennai registrar's office, where my wife-to-be, her best friend Mandira, and I are trying to inch our way through.

Today's mission is to make our wedding legal and binding, obtain a piece of paper that will eventually lead to my getting a lifelong visa, a process that will take years and dozens of trips across Chennai to the legendary FRRO—the Foreign Regional Registration Office.

The lady in charge is sitting at her desk, at the centre of a large room cramped with similar desks and homogenous sari-clad ladies.

The decor has the customary dilapidated bureaucratic flair—pocked leprous walls encrusted with calendars and posters, plus rusty filing cabinets plastered with orders. Not that anyone intends to read or follow any of them.

Only the computer room has an AC, otherwise it's all a whirling and whizzing of fans that do very little to dry this crammed and overheated chamber of hell, filled with hopeful and scared-looking couples, angry mothers and sly brokers who, for a fee, will tell you where to go, who to pay, who to bribe.

'What?!' Mandira screams righteously at one of those fixers, 'Do you see that I am wearing a "Hindu" newspaper badge? Do you understand that I am a journalist? I work for a newspaper? And you are telling me we have to pay a bribe to register a marriage? Really? Really?!'

Mandira does her best to put on her pyrotechnic Kali-gaze, incarnating that dangerous icon called 'the enraged righteous Indian woman', shaking head, hips and all.

The nasal reply from our sleazy, 60-something broker is disarming:

'No, maaadaaam, I am not telling YOU to pay the bribe, I would not do that, of course, how could I? But I'm telling THEM..." as he points his crooked finger towards us, the helpless betrothed. 'I'm telling THEM that if they want to get married they must pay the lady over THERE...'

Now he points to our target, the woman who will decide if we have to come back tomorrow, spend the entire day here or only half an hour and bye-bye.

She's sitting triumphantly on her throne, sanctified by a large poster right behind her, appropriately representing Lakshmi, the goddess of wealth, who exudes coins and banknotes from her very hands.

The bureaucrat also seems to have three sets of arms as she takes care of a couple on her left, through their own busy broker, and a couple on her right, aided by a relative in the transaction.

She grabs official money with a hand and sticks it in the left drawer, after penning the full amount into an archaic register. Then she clasps the bribe money with the other hand and she shoves it straight into the drawer on her right, to be accounted for at the end of the day.

She's now sizing us up with something alternating between contempt and indifference, not a smile, not a moment of humanity: the cold cheek of the State rubbing against our hopes.

*

Sad, but true: in India, big family fortunes are often built on bribes, at one point or another. Months, years, decades of bribes accumulated in corrupted pockets to finally yield the capital necessary to get out and start your business, get a shop or a factory going, get clean and hop over to the other side.

Then you start having to pay bribes to someone else who will come and inspect the premises of your business and tell you that he has had to pay so much money to get to where he is—the job of official extortionist. He's had to get crushed under heavy debt in order to bribe the system into giving him a job where he can exact bribes.

So, please, won't you just play along with the system, be a good spoke of the sacred wheel and pay up, don't make a fuss, don't be uselessly righteous in wanting to change the unchangeable.

Just pay.

'I had to pay to be here asking you to pay,' this is the accepted logic.

But this is unpleasant mostly because there exists, somewhere, somehow an equal aspiration to emancipate a society from this informal taxation system.

In a way, isn't the illegal and yet still popular dowry system a bribe of sort? The mixing of what in theory is a sentimental union with the business side of a possibly life-long partnership? But this deals with the concept of marriage, arranged marriage and passionate unions, which we deal with later.

*

When my Uber driver, while driving me to Phoenix mall in Chennai, gets stopped for a wrong turn, he deserves the ticket he's getting. Yet the traffic officer has an aggressive, very disrespectful attitude towards this entrepreneurial chauffeur.

But it's only because the cop is trying to get 300 rupees in bribes, instead of the more manageable 100.

For someone like this driver, who earns 600 rupees on a good day, it's a considerable amount. But there's no embarrassment or covert gesture to hide the illicit pocketing of the bills.

There's no pretending to give a piece of paper as a receipt for a legal traffic fine. It's all clear, out in the open, under the eyes of the vellai passenger in the back-seat; it's part of life. The wheel of life!

*

When he was only 11, my son Teo had an ambitious dream: manufacturing inexpensive football shoes for young Indian players. He designed them and called them 'The 4 Elements'. Then, with the help and skills of two Italian friends, we got as far as distributing a dozen prototypes to young Indian girls who tested them in Nagaland, Meghalaya, West Bengal, Tamil Nadu, all the way to Ranchi in Jharkhand. They loved them. Fashionable and sturdy.

But when I tried to open a trust company for charitable activities, to manufacture these high quality yet inexpensive football shoes for poor Indian girls, the accountant told me quite clearly that once the office of registration saw foreign names in the founding members list the request for the bribe immediately went up.

Why? There was no hypocrisy about it: because foreigners can pay higher bribes.

I decided not to proceed with this project, for the moment, thinking I should've gotten a Hindu name after all when I got married. Harsh Sadhaka would've been able to pay less almost everywhere. Although, given my freckles and pale Alpine-stock complexion, I'd have to really convince most people I'm a Kashmiri, which in

India is not necessarily better than being catalogued as an Italian.

Even after Sonia Gandhi left power, I mean.

Speaking of Italy, I'm convinced that, by comparison, the Indian bribing system is more efficient than the Italian one because in India it is, yes, possible, but quite unlikely that you'll find someone who gets offended if you offer a bribe and reports you to the police.

Maybe it does happen, I've just never heard about it.

But in Italy—the most corrupt country in Western Europe according to all studies and reports, and also rather competitive with many non-Western countries when it comes to graft—the danger is you might find an honest public officer.

That really is a problem. It makes for an unreliable system: you may be bribing an honest person, who will report you and shut down your business or you may be bribing the wrong person who does not belong to the powerful *famiglia* that really gets things done and you'll have to re-bribe someone else, exposing yourself financially.

*

In India, the bribe is much more accepted socially. The distance between the disdain expressed publicly among Westerners and Westernised-Indians and reality is much further away than in Italy, where the public condemnation of corruption is a business that many intellectuals, writers, journalists and crusaders have built careers on.

The international investors or businessmen I met in Milan, Vicenza, London, New York, Hong Kong, Bangkok or Singapore, when asked what it's like for them to do business with India have inevitably replied: 'Difficult.'

India is no doubt amongst the most unethical places to do business in the world today. The concept of good faith in negotiations is risible. Legal agreements are not truly binding, thanks to the connivance of authorities and a court system that is often reliably for sale.

The solution? Teaching sage Kautilya's *Arthashastra*, a 2000-year-old Hindu treatise often compared to Machiavelli's *The Prince*, on the art of commerce, war and politics that the Modi government has now imposed on technical institutes and business schools nation-wide. The plan would be to create 'karma managers', who will understand the laws of cause and effect, and will act ethically so they don't reincarnate in a lower rung of existence. Teaching 'Creative accounting 101' would certainly be more useful in this context. And more honest, paradoxically.

Please bear with me and let's look at some numbers, lest I get accused of exaggerating.

The problem starts with civil servants, but doesn't end

there. In 2016, out of 176 countries, India ranked 79th in Transparency International's Corruption Perception Index. In 2017, the same Index pointed to India as the most corrupt nation of 16 Asia Pacific countries.

Almost seven in 10 Indians who have had to deal with public services like police, courts, getting official documents, schools, hospitals, utilities and services admitted having to pay a bribe.

In the 2016 Global Business Ethics Survey, India ended up as the most unethical of 13 major economies, trailing behind places like Brazil and China, not the utmost examples of ethical business.

If you want to look at it positively, in the spirit of our time, we could re-spin it like this: 'India is at the top of the list of 13 major world economies, according to the Global Business Ethics Survey, in the most unethical category! Yayy! No one can beat us!'

But now the corruption is seeping into the private sector. Private sector bank executives are known to demand a 'commission' to award contracts to investment companies. Private equity investor Ramesh Venkataram has written in *The Indian Express* that in one case 'we found that the CEO of a subsidiary had been paid off by the winning bidder for an asset that we were disposing'.

This has been common practice in the public sector in many countries, even in the US, where lobbying and campaign financing is in essence a form of deductible bribing. Once it gets to the private sector, the problem is not double, it's immense.

In 2017, according to Ernst and Young's Asia-Pacific Fraud survey, 78 per cent of Indian businessmen who were surveyed confessed that bribery and corruption occurs widely, and, more importantly, 57 per cent of senior management admitted they would ignore unethical behaviour of employees in order to attain their targets in revenue.

How do you reform something like this?

Difficult, since it's a wide-spread habit that begins at the top, in both government and big businesses, and trickles down to the smallest villages, even the ones on the Coromandel Coast of Tamil Nadu.

*

In the India I know, bribes can take on ritualistic, almost folksy forms. The house where my wife and I live, cocooned on a beach between two fishermen villages, exists thanks to an exchange of capital of sorts that could be considered a bribe.

When it was first built, the sarpanch of the village got in touch through intermediaries to demand a 'contribution'. Nothing official, there's no receipt. But it seems clear that if you do not pay, things might get dicey.

In Italy, that's how the Mafia got started. Here, it's somewhat an accepted part of daily life. An extra tax.

I know because I found myself in the middle of a bit of a risky scene with these local, informal 'tax collectors' in an episode which finally revealed to me a mystery I had been wondering about for years: Why are there so many temples in Southern India and in India in general? The answer may seem obvious at first.

India is the world headquarters of spirituality, after all, right? Hence the overabundance of temples. Sure, possible, even probable.

But with so much poverty, how can they be financed, and why?

Turns out, temples are certainly proof of the deep devotion of the common person in India, a testament to the spiritual side which thrives in the offers to the gods, the *tapas*, the austerities and also the tribute of money to the gods.

But temples can also be the best excuse to extort money from affluent neighbours and distribute it first to the mayor—the sarpanch—and his or her friends, and eventually to some relatives as well.

Temple contributions are one of the best ways to keep the official alcohol and underground moonshine industries thriving. This is where part of the money often ends up, making the administrators of the village merry with inebriated pleasure.

A third temple had been in the making in the village of Paramankeni and all the newly arrived real estate owners along the coastline, the outsiders who had been able to buy acres of land and build on it, were being contacted to contribute to the construction costs.

Our Chettiar neighbours had been tapped, the Kalki-One World Academy Ashram for hedge-fund managers had been asked, the Christian centre up the road too and so had the gated Pearl's Beach, Belle Rive and Calm Waters estates with all those euphemistic names hiding the fact that you will get mice and rats invading your house, you might find snakes in your kitchen and in your lawn, the tsunami will come and wipe away your foundations, while floods and cyclones will batter whatever's left from the constant erosion of sea salt and sea winds.

So here we were, my in-laws, my wife and my son, enjoying a relaxing summer weekend at the house when Ammu, the caretaker, comes knocking at the door.

A group of men are marching in the courtyard, demanding to speak to my father-in-law who scuttles into hiding in the shadows by the staircase, making sure not to walk by any window, which could confirm his presence to the uninvited guests.

He quickly whispers to me that it would be wiser, in that specific predicament, for me to go out and discuss things with the brawny fishermen and find out what the locals need from us.

Him being Indian and they knowing he is the one

who financed the building of the house, it would be easier for them to make higher demands from him directly. This is the rationale.

If the aloof vellai who doesn't speak Tamil faces them with his odd foreign ways, the thing might, just might, play out to our advantage.

Or not.

Well, I've stupidly never been someone to turn down the chance to get an adrenaline jolt, unless it's guaranteed you will simply get pummelled, so I march on out to face the fishermen's posse.

There are eight of them, wearing white or checkered lungis and black moustaches just like in the worst Kollywood movies.

The sarpanch speaks the best English of the lot, meaning he might know four words. But Ammu, who by now has improved her command of the idiom, mediates our conversation.

'Temple', 'money', 'paying', 'paint', 'village', '*thailaivar*' [politician], '*ille*' [no], '*rombo jaastee*' [too much]—these are the words I seem to make out and understand interspersed by the charming musicality of Tamil.

But, in the rush to shove out in the courtyard the vellai mappillai, I have not been instructed what to reply. So I improvise and manage to tell them I will come to the village the day after at 6 p.m. to visit them and we would discuss 'the needful'.

'Confirmed?' One of them asks, revealing his knowledge of this essential English word.

'Confirmed.'

When I go back to the house, I find my father-in-law still hiding by the staircase and we devise a strategy which can help us contribute to the village without feeding a possible passion for alcohol or other vices—a way to participate, by making sure the contribution will really go to the temple not to the bootlegger.

I've heard so many stories of deals like these gone wrong from friends in Chennai and in other rural communities—residents confronted head on by the villagers and who found themselves surrounded by enraged and drunk farmers with torches and pitchforks.

Literally.

Or taxi drivers from the neighbourhood demanding to be the exclusive drivers of the hotel or ashram, etc. The world-famous Indian lynch mob which, from the enraged posse's point of view, is at times the only way to bypass the possible corruption of some justice venues.

I have my strategy ready when my wife, my disconcerted son and I drive to the village the day after to discuss the proper amount of our voluntary-but-actually-mandatory contribution.

*

Paramenkeni is not a very imposing village.

Quite the contrary, actually.

It's a small fishing town 90 km south of Chennai, on the road to Pondicherry: about a thousand hectares in the Cheyyur Taluk (Cheyyur County) of the Kancheepuram district.

This probably means nothing to you, unless you live around here. It means that in the Paramankeni area there is a colourful little hamlet near a quaint lagoon, looking into the sunset to the West. But there's also another group of little houses, between the Buckingham Canal and the Bay of Bengal facing the sun at dawn, to the East.

The population has doubled since a five-and-a-half metre tsunami wave wiped out 235 houses in the west-facing village on 26 December 2004.

Since then, a couple of German organizations have helped rebuild the village. The Karl Kübel Stiftung project finished 202 houses: 26 with the help of Hessen hilft, 75 with the help of Andheri Hilfe and 101 with the help of Caritas.

Now there are 847 families living here. More women (1710) than men (1615) for a total of 3,325 people according to the latest census. It may actually have grown a bit since then.

It has lower than average literacy rate by Tamil Nadu standards, 65.29 per cent. It means over a third of the people here can't read or write.

Half of them are employed for more than six months out of the year, the other half are involved in so called marginal activity, working for less than six months a year or being unemployed.

Of the 1,500 who are engaged in main work, only 98 of them are owners or co-owners of agricultural land, 78 are labourers. Most others have jobs related to fishing.

As you walk into the perfectly rectangular dawn-facing village, set between high cement walls, now at a safe distance from the sea, what strikes you is how un-Indian the urban plan is. It looks more like an ancient Roman *castrum*, a military fortress with its main street or *Via Praetoria* intersected perfectly by its *Via Principalis*, to create a cross and six smaller streets crossing at precise 90-degree gradients, with a large square at the centre.

All very angular, must have been that German rationality at work, rebuilding the tsunami-ravaged village. Or more likely it was inspired by the square plan of the Chola temples.

As you stroll through Paramenkeni, you will see fishermen squatting in front of their purple, yellow or green homes mending nets, farmers drying crops, a bright little candy and snacks store in one corner, washed in the sunset light, children playing cricket, a lady pumping water out of a mechanical well. Here and there, very nourishing little fish drying in the sun, on a bed of thin sticks.

Let's hope tourists never discover this.

Please *do not* come visit.

Thank you.

It always reminds me of an Asterix comic book coming to life, although I'm beginning to look more like Obelix whenever I wander around here surrounded by the multifarious saris, the striped lungis and wrap-around turbans, in this most elegant rural setting. India, the best-dressed poor people in the globe, really.

Perfect spot for cheesy Orientalism.

This time, as I get out of the vehicle with wife and son, I sport my widest and best smile, still not knowing what awaits.

Then, as we're ushered into the temple grounds, I proceed to nonchalantly tour the premises by going around the building and returning to a large crowd of fishermen who, after asking us to sit on plastic armchairs, right smack in the middle of the white temple, while the crowd sits at our feet all around us, proceed to list their requests.

First, they expose their demands kindly in a Tamil that both Ammu and my wife try to translate to me. Then, one raises his voice somewhat menacingly it seems. Someone else seems to agree and raises his voice even higher.

It does not look good. I can't understand a thing, I decide to keep my best smile on and tell Ammu to announce our plan.

Paint.

We'll buy some paint for the temple.

And we'll deliver it before the monsoon.

I don't know how you say 'hooray' in Tamil but the buzzing and brouhaha going through the crowd indicates most people are convinced it is actually a good idea.

The sarpanch also looks convinced or forced to accept that it might be a good solution. One solitary, not very bright looking older fisherman even claps loudly for what seem like many embarrassing seconds, as the cool-hearted Tamil fishermen do not seem to follow up but appear to nod some measure of approval.

We've just found a way to bribe without bribing, to give back to the community we actually didn't really belong to, except for a real estate presence, and we just might have gotten away with it.

Of course, the contradiction also dawns on us that we are indirectly financing a temple that will now blast its loudspeakers into our ears, ruining the isolated quality of life we've enjoyed until now.

Blame it on the Muslims, of course. Apparently, it all started when the muezzins invested in new technologies to call to prayer from the minarets. And you have those Christians with their obsessions for bells, on the other hand.

So Hindus, not to be outdone, got into the market of loudspeakers where you can hear Bollywood songs reminding Hindus to stay Hindu.

*

The epilogue to this story is that a few months later, our racketeering, benevolent extortionist neighbours come to visit again. They are not happy with our handyman's offer to deliver paint for the entire ceiling of the temple.

'Not enough' is the message delivered by the fabulous eight who reappear on our courtyard, sleeves rolled up, checkered lungi and all. Not enough.

'So, what does that mean?' I ask, trying to see if they might formulate a threat.

'You are part of our village, this is your way to participate, to show you appreciate being here,' the smiling leader of this expedition says.

'Of course, I love being in Paramenkeni,' I reply, 'and I love Paramankeni, that's beyond the point. But my wife and I are just writers. We don't have staff, as you can see, aside from Ammu. We cook our meals, we wash our clothes. We write books, we don't have factories like our neighbours, we don't have wealthy, paying foreign guests, like the ashrams. I know I am a vellai, but I live here and I earn in rupees.'

'But 25 thousand rupees is not enough,' they insist.

'But that is what the factory owners and the ashram owners have paid!' I try to reason.

'I know, but just a little bit more...' says a smiling man, accompanied by the many smiles of the other seven clean looking, decent-person faces of the gang.

My wife and I look at each other. We have just paid

the gardener to plant new crops for our vegetable garden, Ammu's salary, the electricity repair after the latest storm has flared up a cable as thick as a banana, and we are slightly out of pocket at the moment.

And yet, it would've been easier to manage an angry crowd waving pitchforks somehow, than these smiling sets of teeth. The disarming simplicity of these twinkling men, the kind blackmailers who are simply asking for a little bit more by pinching the air between their thumb and index fingers. The fastidious anger subsides and leaves room for the very Indian desire for harmony.

'Your job is to have fun,' my adorable father-in-law had told us as he waved goodbye from the house, when we had left Chennai a few days before.

What are 15 thousand more rupees? A lot, actually, in this specific moment. But it's the best way to close this anecdote.

We agree on 40 thousand, cash, no paint, just those smirking Gandhi notes that they could use to drink themselves silly, even though they promise to provide receipts. I mean, it's 500 euros, 620 dollars, 440 pounds: the exact median annual per-capita income in India!

Hey, they'll even write our names as contributors on the temple walls at inauguration in May, they swear. We have reached a compromise, which means a point at which both parties are ok with it but both also slightly unsatisfied by the result.

I did ask for one condition: that they pose for the official picture of our agreement to which they immediately comply by happily giving me a very memorable image, of a middle-aged European, a bit overheated and puffy faced from being too long in the sun debating with fishermen, wearing such an inelegant sweat spotted t-shirt, grubby running shorts and old flip flops, shaking hands with the leader of a group of picture-perfect shirted and lungi-sporting fishermen who'd just extorted 40 thousand rupees for their temple.

Smile, click!

*

As you can see, one way or another, just like the cost of living goes up, Indian bribes also find a way not only to elude instrumental political campaign to eradicate them, but they also manage to increase with time.

Back in Chennai, at a function I run into a European man who's also married to a lovely young woman from Madras and who owns a big factory in Tamil Nadu.

I ask him about the new government.

'I heard things in Delhi are running more efficiently now. Bureaucrats are asked to be at their desk on time,' I say. 'And it seems to be working. No inefficient bureaucracy, so they say. I mean, have you experienced this? Has bribing disappeared or at least gotten lighter, more difficult, less demanding?'

'Quite the contrary, it's gotten more expensive,' the businessman says surprisingly, as he proceeds to reveal an interesting mechanism that has been established in the bribing world of India.

'You see, before this new government came to power I had to pay directly to every single person involved in the process, all the way down to the smallest pawn. Now that Modi had set up this Mussolini-like system of control, intimidating officials into not giving in to corruption, I only have to give one bribe.'

'Oh, well, you see, so you are paying less, after all, right?' I comment, naively. 'Only one bribe!'

'No, actually...no. Here's how it works now: since checks and inspections are more severe, it is less risky to just pay one person, once. So I have to pay the top guy the entire sum I would normally distribute to everyone. And, then, he distributes it to all the others. Just like before. I mean everyone still gets a cut.'

'So, why isn't it less costly? Or, at least, it should be as expensive as before, right? Not more...'

'Well, no, because the top guy or the top lady is now charging a distribution fee, you see? I have to pay more for the service of him or her internally paying everyone else down the line. So, you see, all in all it's become more expensive than before!'

Driving with Hitler before walking into Stalin

Or total absence of humour renders life impossible

As I get in the car waiting for me outside the house in Chennai early in the morning, I greet the driver and instinctively glance at his name plate. We're going to be riding together in the same intimate cubicle of the Innova until after sunset, so we may as well know each other's name from the start.

The permit reads: 'Driver name: John Hitler.'

I can't keep my mouth shut.

'So, John Hitler...hmm...is that a first *and* last name?'

'No, no,' the kind man with a (yes!) tooth-brush moustache says. 'That is first name. John Hitler, only first name.'

'I see, and who decided to call you Hitler? Was it your mother? Your father, perhaps? Someone else in the family interested in German history?'

I proceed with caution, weighed down by my own experience with this name, having been born only 21 years after the other Hitler's death, and in Geneva, not that far from where he died, and having grown up with this name being the symbol of ultimate evil.

'No, no, Hitler, second name only. It was parish priest.'

'Oh, the parish priest, really?' I prod. 'And why?'

'He said Hitler very good terror name. Very good frightening name!' he smiles.

'You do have a point there,' I conclude and we let the subject rest for the rest of our ride.

In the seat next to me there's my friend, the historian William Dalrymple. We share the same birthday which is why we address each other as 'Zodiac Bro'. We're heading to Gingee Fort and then to other historic sites which are the settings of his next book and I want to take in some Tamil countryside.

John Hitler takes us out of that imbroglio of metal and asphalt that is trying to get out of Chennai on any day. Finally, a clear stretch of highway and we whiz down to our destination where we climb the ancient fort conquered by Muslims, Hindus, French, and Britons.

'Aaah, I just love India!' exclaims my Zodiac Bro, with his characteristic emotional enthusiasm.

We catch our breath once we've finally reached the summit and can observe the dreamy paddy fields caressed by the wind like ruffled hair.

We are ruined by culture, so for me it is inevitable to conjure up Satyajit Ray and his 'Apu' waiting for that train out in the fields, can't escape that representational view of the Indian countryside from up here. Although I'm fully aware we're not in West Bengal. And this is not in black and white. It's in full multi-chrome Indian masala for the eyes.

William is ecstatic.

'Should we add this to our empire?' he jokes, looking out into the hills and fields of Tamil Nadu.

'Our empire is built on words, so this is already ours,' I pontificate, repenting immediately for my know-it-all tendencies.

We are ruined by culture. There goes spontaneity.

John Hitler pedals to the metal for another two hours until we reach Arcot, where that British *conquistador* known as Robert Clive, stood his ground in a major battle.

Then we head back north, in this tour of 'Tamil Nadu in a day', searching for two obelisks commemorating the death of hundreds of Brits in the battle of Pullulur.

It is already dusk. And then sunset. And now it is pitch dark.

In the village, they tell us to take a little road that ends in paddy fields and where it is difficult for John Hitler to manoeuvre a three-point turn around to get us out.

William is distraught. We arrived too late. Can't find the place.

I've always had good night vision and I sense that somewhere out there, south-west from where we are stuck near a farm, there could be something.

John Hitler and William don't see a thing. But they decide to trust my shamanic night vision powers.

The two dilapidated obelisks are actually where I said they'd be, much to William's surprise. We ask John Hitler to keep the headlights on, shining some luminosity on the cement being conquered by plants, already gripping the memorial to the British soldiers who got ambushed, stood their ground, but lost their lives here.

William is taken as in a dream by these visions of the past. It is as if he could see them.

I am more curious about the family who lives in this farm, right next to this totem no one clearly has visited for years, and what they must think of these two vellais, showing up in the middle of the night just to read some inscriptions on the useless slabs of cement next to their fields. Are they proud of their ancestors being able to squash that first invasion and to kill so many Brits?

Apparently there's not much interest in these sort of questions among the farmer communities in Tamil Nadu. What do they care about? Most likely they care about produce prices, working conditions, poor quality of roads, but even more likely about Superstar Rajinikanth, wondering whether or not he'll run for chief minister. Or thinking about the latest Kollywood flick. Not the dreams of history, but the reveries of cinema.

It's time to return to the wrestling embrace of Chennai traffic, inching our way back into the monster and celebrate with a great South Indian dinner.

As we drive back I study some of the bumper stickers

and signs—one of the most entertaining activities in India. I keep a mental collection of my favourites, in my years of riding and driving around India.

There's the conscious witticism, the heavy handed deadpan jokes and the world of misspelling and advertisement.

So when the YWCA of Delhi announces in capital letters in front of their building that 'TOTAL ABSENCE OF HUMOUR RENDERS LIFE IMPOSSIBLE', I can't refrain from saying out loud: 'Exactly!'

These are the roads where you may find a cheerful bus announcing it is 'Propeld By Clean Fuel'. But if you have to make a pit stop, in a bathroom you may find a poster that reminds that the common aim is 'to keep this bathroom clean', and in order to do so it proceeds to warn each gender:

'Ladies Please remain seated during entire performance!' and

'Gentleman Your aim will help! Stand closer. It's shorter than you think.'

As you drive by a government building, you may notice two smiling ladies next to a sign that warns you to 'Please Take Off Arms Before Enter'.

And if you want to get a haircut you can find a 'Decent Hair Parlour' and a 'Faision Haircutting' in so many small towns like the ones John Hitler is driving us through.

When the time comes, you can stop and try the 'Indian Chaines Fast Food' in a restaurant called 'Hotel Something Special'. And I know how they feel in that Kodai restaurant called 'Amma Mess'.

But I still don't understand why, in Kodaikkanal, they would call a restaurant 'Orendo', considering the horrendous service I've experienced there.

When waiters don't accept your ragged rupees, you can take your Gandhi notes to the bank where a sign reassures you that 'Mutilated notes are exchanged here'.

If you think, erroneously, all this happens only because some people didn't study English properly, you can always sign up for a course. Look over there, there's a neon sign reminding you of an Institute of English Language called, yes, 'Speakwel'.

*

I wake up early the next morning, back in the guest room where I stay in Besant Nagar, at my in-laws' house. Too late to get back to sleep, but too early to get up and go for the morning walk at the Theosophical Society where I regularly run into Stalin and his eight body guards.

Stalin is the son of a former chief minister and political legend of Tamil Nadu, M. Karunanidhi. This moustachioed stroller, nodding back at me while being followed by his toughies, is who everyone thinks will be the next leader of this state.

I sit in the temporary silence of a room facing a residential neighbourhood which is increasingly becoming noisier. Not just the usual firecracker funeral, or the Dalits with their trash bins coming to collect and chat with Munni—the Tamil caretaker and painter who lives in the garage.

More and more cars are now driving through the street searching for a new shortcut to avoid traffic.

Blame it on Google Maps.

I stare at the fan swirling slowly on the ceiling and in the stillness I think I'm almost hearing the famous watch still ticking on MGR's wrist, deep inside the mausoleum where the legendary chief minister movie star rests in Marina Beach. Now MGR is flanked by a new mausoleum, that of former chief minister (and his mistress), Jayalalitha, recently departed after a brief stint in jail for fraud.

What do Stalin's father Karunanidhi, M.G. Ramachandran and Jayalalitha have in common, aside from having all been chief ministers of independent India's Tamil Nadu?

They were working together in the same business of dreams: cinema. Karunanidhi was the scriptwriter. MGR the star. Jayalalitha the rising singing and dancing starlet. They have been venerated like gods and goddesses; raising the legitimate question that God may be an actor himself. Or herself.

Power and cinema, an inevitable twist in this picturesque Tamil Nadu. Reality and cinema, another unavoidable relationship as I am to discover that same night as my wife and I decide to drive to watch a movie at Phoenix Mall.

ᴕ

We are going to watch a Tamil language movie called *Madras*. Tishani's cousin, Apeksha, and her husband, Kunal, have kindly offered to help with the translation since there are no subtitles.

I love the sound of Tamil, the most ancient spoken language. But I don't understand it. Blame it on my age, on the objective intricacies of this idiom, the point is: 'Tamil ille!' I just don't get it.

As I turn left at a traffic light, I suddenly have to step on the brakes because there's a little crowd following a flower-draped chariot. We inch slowly behind it, as we start to hear familiar jolly drums and we're allowed to coast around on the right side, as we watch the customary dances around the funeral procession. The bangs, the frizzling fire crackers, the songs—these chants and screams among the laughter always bring to mind a similar procession I saw as a teenager in New Orleans: 'Oh When the Saint's Go Marching In.'

At that moment, I couldn't know that funeral procession had an odd connection to the movie we were about to watch.

Madras (SPOILER ALERT!) is a love story in the midst of gang turf wars in a North Chennai middle class neighbourhood. There's the Romeo and Juliet tale of the girl who belongs to a different gang's territory. There's the classic Indian bromance between the lead character (impersonated by Tamil star Karthi) and the very well played expendable friend who gets caught in an unhealthy row with his own local political boss.

Best friend takes the fall for lead character. Gets hacked with sickles and axes at the entrance of the court, where he was to be arraigned under suspicion of a murder he did not commit. Turns out the murdered young man is actually a victim of inside politics cloaked by a revenge motive. Confused? Good.

To end the movie, there's a dancing funeral for the expendable friend, and much more battling, scuffling, switching sides, betrayal of alliances, before the movie ends on a sour note and with the lesson (literally on a blackboard, yes, with a little chalk marker in hand) being taught to children about the need to always question authority.

During intermission we are shown an odd commercial. A girl is drawing a picture of a mother-bird feeding a worm with her beak to little birds in their nests. The girl is interrupted by her mother who stuffs a fistful of rice down the girl's throat, a common practice in these parts—hand feeding grown-up kids. Then, we suddenly see Jayalalitha, Amma, the chief minister, distributing free rice bags to her followers.

I don't know if the allegory is clear enough to you: politician feeds mothers bags of rice; mothers feed that rice to their children. It's the way things are, it's natural, just like mother bird feeds her birdies in the nest.

This is politics in Tamil Nadu. Take the rice, gimme the vote (although rice-bag political bribes have through the years escalated to toasters, TVs, and now, I imagine, to cheap smartphones).

Yet, the real surprise is waiting in the morning newspaper, the morning after, as I sit in the hot Rukmani Road veranda before our sacred breakfast.

The Hindu tells me that the funeral we saw on the way to the movie was that of a victim hacked to death. Just like in the movie. The headline: 'AIADMK functionary murdered.' Subtitle: 'Attacked by gang; Police suspect business rivalry as motive.' The killing happened in Velachery—the neighbourhood of the Luxe movie theatre.

A young politician was hacked to death at dawn on the day we drove to the movies in his neighbourhood, in order to watch a movie about a young political functionary being hacked to death by a gang of killers armed with knives and sickles.

'In public view on Tuesday morning, an armed gang hacked a 43-year-old AIADMK functionary to death.

He was just a few streets away from his home when a four-member gang that was waiting for him ran in and attacked him brutally with knives and sickles in front of passersby who immediately fled in fear.'

Apparently the motivation was money. His wife, says the article, 'Is a money-lender in the area and [her husband] often made the daily money collections on her behalf.'

The police told the newspaper that 'the couple's money-lending activity could have gained them a few rivals in the form of ex-clients who allegedly lost huge amounts of money and even their homes due to exorbitant interest rates. The case is being investigated to determine if the murder was orchestrated by one of the clients or if it was politically motivated, the police said.'

As I fold the newspaper, with a slight shudder, I ask myself if I wasn't better off not knowing about this aspect of Tamil reality.

Lost in my hazy ideal on this corner of South India, with its snail-speed traffic, its wailing, enchanted temples, its incense and flowery fragrances mixed with overflowing monsoon sewers, the elegant saris, the stylish lungis, now that I let curiosity lead me here, I wonder if it's not preferable to imagine and dream, instead of discovering some uglier realities.

My answer is: No.

SEX, RACISM, IDENTITY, BUT MOSTLY MANGOS!

Discovering the vengeful meaning of British colonial clubs while sipping British Empire, being mansplained about the dirty shades of the crisis of puritanism, facing the fact that I may have now become an uncle who finds out what happens when hotties become aunties.

'I am the best mango!'

Or a tropical fruit's role in parochialism and identity in India

'Indians and Dogs not Allowed.'

Signs at the entrance, as many Indians bitterly remember, used to really say that.

Colonial era clubs are places that many of the current members' grandfathers were shooed off from, barred entrance, pushed off as unwelcome nuisances.

These exclusive expats' reservations were off limits to the browner race. It seems only logical that the real revenge for many contemporary Indians is to be able to be here sporting nice loafers bought on that last trip to London, buttondown shirts purchased at the Brooks Brothers franchise in Phoenix Mall or showing off an expensive Swiss watch.

I've often asked myself why these clubs are still standing, why Indians in major cities don't build new homes for the aggregation of power, new backdrops for that very human act of seeking exclusivity while networking, eating, drinking cocktails or throwing some sort of a ball across a field divided by a net.

While sipping an appropriately named British Empire beer, lounging under a wall plastered with bronze and wooden plaques commemorating the names of Anglo-Saxon administrators, I can't help smiling to myself at the secret agenda behind members who chose this kind of a place to mingle, as a historic revenge against the symbols of the power that once enslaved their ancestors.

In Chennai, the Madras Club is the apex; although the Cricket Club's up-and-coming business leaders consider it a den of old fogeys, while the Boat Club might be regarded as a notch down, but it is pleasantly less formal. The Gymkhana Club has been festooned with hammer and sickle red flags of striking workers for months.

Today is baby Rudra's first birthday party. His parents, tennis semi-pros Rajeev and Sai, have decided to celebrate it at the Cricket Club.

I'm lost in these thoughts about identity when I run into my new friend Somdev Devvarman, an international tennis champion built like a jock with a contagious smile and a doer attitude, who introduces me to his girlfriend, a gracious and cute law student from Pune.

Her eyes dart around the room and she's no slow talker. Finally, her gaze falls on me, this strange vellai in a room full of Indians in a British colonial club. She shoots out all her curiosity in a volley of questions.

'What are you doing here? How long have you been in India? Don't you miss Europe? Or the US?'

As I attempt the most honest answers I can muster, she laughs, having noticed I unknowingly adopt the

Indian head bob. I'm even doing the horizontal wrist twist, at this point.

'Wait, wait,' she says, 'now I get it, I understand…'

'What?' I ask.

'I understand what you are.'

'What *I* am?'

'Yes.'

'What *am* I?'

'You are a reverse coconut.'

'A what?'

Somdev, who's lived in the States and has a better American accent than mine, interjects and explains.

'See, a coconut is the name used for an Indian who's been in the West so long that he's actually brown on the outside and white on the inside,' Somdev says. 'So she's saying you are a reverse coconut: white on the outside, Indian on the inside.'

*

When I was studying intercultural communication with Professor Gary Weaver at The American University in Washington D.C. in 1986, I remember we analyzed one of the psychological threats posed by intercultural relations.

'It is called "going native",' the charismatic, bearded Professor Weaver explained to an enraptured class. 'Adopting the clothes and customs of the locals, their language, accent and mannerism. Losing your identity, who you have been up until that point, in order to be accepted and integrated. Trying to look like the locals in order to be loved by them.'

At the baby's birthday party, I look over at Radha, a kind-hearted 80-year-old friend who's taken me to see classical Indian dance performances at the Kalakshetra Dance Academy, bakes delicious bread, and makes top-notch Malayali dishes learned from her husband's family. She might look more like the example of going native, I think.

Her full name is Radha Gopalakrishnan and she's one of the most adorable people I know in Chennai. She always wears a dashing sari, keeps her long, pretty white hair in a braid, never lost a trace of Irish accent mixed with an Indian twang.

From Catholicism, she converted to Hinduism taking a Hindu name and then, after accidentally finding herself in a private audience with the Dalai Lama in Dharmashala, became a devout Buddhist, taking care of the Buddhist temple at the Theosophical Society, where I meet her regularly on evening walks, right past the grand tree planted by Jiddu Krishnamurti.

And I think of my own mother-in-law, who doesn't strike me as a 'reverse coconut' at all. Although she's been here just as long as Radha, over 40 years, she seems like the example of someone who, even though she's mastered the culture and cuisine she's moved into, has remained deeply Welsh. She has a brilliant and witty sense of humour, forever youthful in good looks and lively spirit. Yet, in a purely Welsh sort of way. Not all vellais react alike to India.

Identity. Who are we?

Who are these people who belong to my nomadic tribe; the expats, the European migrants, the vellais, the goras?

The Irish, English, Welsh ladies married to the Malayali, Sindhi or Gujarati gentlemen who comprise the tribe of friends traveling all together with my mixed marriage in-laws?

What is their identity and how do you define it?

The simple answer would be that there's no such thing as identity.

Am I a reverse coconut?

I don't know.

But I know that once I spent two full years in India and Asia without escaping back to the West, I stopped being one of those winter tourists, one of them Europeans or Americans, Canadians, Australians who spend the cooler months in India, from, say, November to March and then rush back to the real seasons in their semi-organized, orderly societies.

It is only then, that I finally earned this new label.

*

It takes a mango to turn you into a coconut

There is one specific experience that has allowed me to become this. It happened thanks to a thing. A living thing. An organic object of the edible kind.

It's yellow, yet pinkish, but orange.

It's an ovate, and yet a round fibrous thing.

You got it: mango!

Being in India through mango season, starting in late March until mid-August, is the real test of a reverse coconut.

It takes a mango to turn you into a coconut.

I warned you I'm a lunatic.

April, May. These are the unbearably hottest months, especially in Tamil Nadu.

Agni Nakshatram days. Even the most weathered Tamil person I know admits there's a real change of lifestyle imposed by the pressure of that incandescent disc in the sky, Surya—the Sun God—up there in the heavens burning brown the edges of leaves, aided by the breath of the hot southern wind just when in the sky you can see the star of the Fire God—Agni Nakshatram—and the hot wind comes to take away the weakest.

What kind of seasons do we get in Tamil Nadu, you ask?

'Hot, hotter, hottest,' is the answer, yes.

Hottest means summer—April and May—when the air is always heavy with moisture, the breeze becomes a lost hope and time stands still in evenings wrapped in lethargic gloom as everything seems to be melting into itself.

I spend these summer days exiled in AC life. Once I get home to Rukmani Road in an AC car, I run through the garage, up the stairs, straight into the bedroom-studio, already sweating, hoping the air conditioner has already been turned on. I wipe my forehead and stand still in bed with a computer, right under the blowing freon gas wind.

When I run out of water, I stare at the closed door. I know I'll have to yank it open and face the familiar wall of heat. It's right there, clawing at the door handle on the other side.

I can almost smell it. Yet I must hydrate.

So, as I swing the door open, there it is, as unbelievably damp as when I left it, engulfing every inch of my skin.

It's an entity, a thing, a state of being.

The marble floor beneath my bare feet is hot, the wood of the table under my fingers is hot, the metal faucet I twist open is hot, the button of the water filter I press is hot, the filled water bottles I touch are hot. I'll let you guess what the air I breathe feels like in nostrils and lungs.

If you haven't experienced it, it's hard to believe. It's got nothing to do with those hot European summers, those hot New York summer days, nor those burning hot and humid Gulf of Mexico days or the Cuban, Colombian, Brazilian summers I've experienced.

I feel like I have a limited autonomy, before my thinking loses focus, my feet start dragging, small lakes of sweat appear under armpits, chest and neck, as I drag myself back to the room clutching the water bottle, donning a crown of sweaty pearls on my forehead, King Carlo of Heatdom!

Those who can afford it, survive summers in the sterile environment of filtered air. The AC hotel bars, AC restaurants, AC shopping malls, AC movie theatres, unless they are able to run up to the hill stations, the Kodaikanals, the Ootys, the Himalayas, a higher altitude relief from unbreathable air.

And yet, once, I tried to see what it feels like to take a walk at noon in midtown Chennai in a hot, end of April day. Just to experience what the locals go through. And to ascertain I'd survive it; an extreme experience of sorts.

The sun was pushing through my UVA-proof cap, melting my brain into my eyes, liquefying into my mouth while the whole mess dissolved into the neck, disintegrated into my shoulders, as everything percolated in a constant fountain of sweat onto my feet glued to chappals barely able to unstick their rubber soles from the asphalt, while the road seemed to be fading into the sidewalks, creeping along with the heat into the stores, the banks, the hairdressers' salons and the food carts selling plates of rice and dal to Tamil folks dipping the tips of their welded fingers into juicy carbs fuming in the heat.

Summer. The real test of your Indianization is to pull through this season without going insane. It's an unspoken rule, but it is clear.

There is a sort of enhanced respect you will get from people who've grown up through these summers, if you endure this season here.

You're no longer a tourist coming to use India to soothe your occidental neuroses and escape the winter cold. You are not just a weirdo escaping your own weirdness in a distant, exotic land.

You have now melted into a proper reverse coconut.

And so, now, you deserve to really understand the meaning of mango.

Many Indians I know speak about mangoes like some Italians or French discuss wines. Aroma, odour, flavour, sweetness, sourness, raisin-like feeling, tenderness, fibrousness and after-taste. And regional pride. All dissected in detail.

Impossible to find consensus. 'Just wait until you taste _____ (pen in your favourite mango type). Then you'll tell me which one is really the best mango!'

It will happen. Langra, Ratol, Banganpalli, Alphonso, etc.

If you've grown up in Maharashtra it might be this one.

If you're from Bihar it's more likely to be another one.

If you're from Tamil Nadu you'll swear it's most likely Banganpalli, but then your Gujju husband will get his seasonal box of Alphonso mangoes and the argument will start.

The association of your identity with the mango is clear. It's not that you have the best mango. You *are* the best mango.

Preference is born out of association with the emotions of the formative years, although this can change as you grow up. Wine is an acquired taste you may develop in adolescence in certain parts of Europe. In India, you go from suckling the maternal teat to sucking on mango stones.

I'd say it's purely Freudian, if old Sigmund hadn't been almost entirely disqualified as a quack by most contemporary psychologists.

*

I had my first alcoholic drink early on, in my native town of Valdagno. My first beer in 7th grade, while having pizza with friends at the Luna Rossa pizzeria where, in 1978, no one thought that letting a table of young boys and girls share two large bottles of ale on a Saturday night would hurt any one.

I learned about wine a few years later, when I was around 15, but only began to appreciate it in my 20s.

When I had my first sip, I felt like I'd shoved a spoon-full of pure denatured alcohol in my mouth. I didn't puke right away, but it was a disgusting mixture which I slowly grew to like.

You learn to appreciate the nuances, but it's a learning process you first have to force yourself into. It's not an immediate one but a cultivated experience.

Instead, mango is clearly a childhood Proustian madeleine for those lucky enough to be raised in mango-land. The 'mango divide' continues between husband and wife from the first confessions of preference, possibly during courtship and engagement, and continues until one of the spouses either divorces or becomes a widow. And, again, there are exceptions, like the one that my friends Ambarish and Ruma Satwik articulated so well for me.

I transcribe their analysis to prove my previous points on the obsession for the art of the mango.

Indians talking about mango: a sample.

Ruma: 'I have to admit that our current favourites are not what we grew up with. I grew up eating mostly three varieties of mangoes—the Dussheri, the Langada and the Chausa. Totaparis and Sindooris would sometimes find their way in but only because there was nothing else available in the market.

'I would love the Langda the most. I believe it is grown all over UP and North India. It has an attractive green colour, is never as sweet or fibrous as the Dussheri, has a distinct mango smell that reminds me of childhood and most importantly it has a slight hint of sourness as you reach the skin when eating a slice. This distinct sweet sourness and its smell I guess are what I like about it.

'However, now, the Ratol has quickly replaced Langda in the number 1 spot. We were introduced to it about four years ago. According to me, it's the Langda, enhanced three times over. Ambarish has also switched loyalties from Alphonso to Ratol. But maybe he could tell you why.'

Ambarish: 'Yes, mango cultivar chauvinism comes from a familial and social rendering of Proust's madeleine. The degustation of mangoes is the remembrance of things past, the taste of memory. It's also a matter of the family legislating connoisseurship. Offspring are always bred on the familial favourite and then from there, like the first kiss, subsequent variants are always measured by it.

'For the Hapus (Alphonso) bred, the colour of his mangoes is the colour of the areolae of nubile Konkani women: gold and saffron. For him the Dussehris will always be anaemic, even the ones from Malihabad, the flesh not quite as gamy. The Langda will be lame, the Safeda a caricature, the Fazli a mutant. The Kesar munching Gujarati will commonly derogate green or greenish pellicles. Other mangoes will be inadequate in their yellowness or ovate and not the right kind of teardrop paisley. For the Andhraite, as you said, the Banganpalli is the blockbuster, though it's not half as euphonic as the Pakistani Lab-e-Mashooq or Jannat-ul-Firdaus.

'The Pakistani artist Bani Abidi has a wonderful video piece about mango chauvinism. Two friends, a Pakistani and an Indian (both played by the artist) sit together and eat mangoes. They talk nostalgically and effusively about their growing up years, but their recounting gets increasingly agonistic when they start comparing mangoes. The video is meant to allegorize nuclear warheads and one-upmanship. The aside it delivers is how mangoes are an important prop to identity.'

If you're a vellai or a gora you will not immediately get what this is all about. Until you spend a summer here.

Only then you will experience that fructose-induced well being from the mango pulp melting in your mouth, reaching deeply into your emotional state of mind, which through the years will make you talk about mangoes like Ruma and Ambarish.

Then you will understand, by studying mango-talk, that mango preference is not divided necessarily among nuclear family lines. The type of mango you prefer is connected to the family and place where you grew up. And then it evolves, through research, exploration, experiment. It builds a history of taste. And this reflects your evolution, your nomadic transmigration from one mango-territory to the next.

So when my otherwise respectable and reasonable friend Dr Vikrom Mathur, on a hot June afternoon in Delhi, in the middle of his sun filled living room in Nizamuddin, begins to swear 'I have the best mango!' excitedly like the adorable little bully he can be, what he is trying to say is 'I *am* the best mango,' as the mango-sweet ego-thumping Dilliwalla that he is, of course.

You are the Alphonso, the Banganpalli, the Ratol.

This is what you grew up with.

Or what you discovered and decided to identify with.

This is what you are.

And this is why you think: it's the best fruit in the world. Because for you it was, when you were four or five or even younger. Or when you changed and became the new you.

It's also because you think that you, just like your mango, are the best thing in the world.

It's called the mango ego-imprint.

The fifty shades of red in India's Fabindia

Or retail masochism for housewives among the Not-So-New-Indians

There must be at least 30 friends gathered around Harri for his birthday party at the Park Hyatt in Chennai tonight. Dirty Harry was given his nickname because his generous heart is too big for only one girl.

He's now my best friend in Chennai, a man with a soul as large as his roaring laughter, as solid as the cement he deals in, and as wild as the rave parties he's rocked.

I think of him when people say: 'You come to India with a plan, but India has a plan for you.'

When a Palestinian friend and his girlfriend landed in Chennai for their first visit to India, Harri sent them a driver in a private car furbished with a funky little box containing the finest Himalayan sweets to make their drive to the house all the more joyful and pleasant. Later we all got lost in the meandering alleys of Mylapore, getting dragged into total strangers' weddings, as we exited the temple.

That is the kind of plan India sometimes has for you.

Tonight the plan is to celebrate this dude.

A lanky lady from Quebec, who says she's French, is singing '80s covers. The usual buffet of tired skewers and rubbery paneer cubes absorb the alcoholic intake. Guests wander into the courtyard's pool, gathering around a giant Ganesh statue indifferent to all the smoking, drinking and chatting.

This party is on a middle ground between the moralizing Modi-fied India, angry at any public display of affection (PDA), juxtaposed with the India of the jeans-clad militant kiss-mobs, the 20-something love crusaders slobbering into each others' mouths to affirm their right to do such things in public. No PDA!

I'm now surrounded by an upper middle class India that is discovering a new relationship with its body and its sexuality. A very interesting, privileged India I'm happy to belong to, first as a curious outsider, and slowly as an almost integrated foreign appendix.

Unexpectedly, the man sitting next to me, Sunil, blurts out in one breath the whole plot of the *50 Shades of Grey* trilogy.

'It is not an erotic book,' he insists, staring at me to check if I dare to disagree, 'it is literature!'

Is that a feminist gleam in his eyes as, SPOILER ALERT, he explains that the sadomasochistic game stops in the first book?

'In the following one, she makes him fall in love with her and they get married,' Sunil says. 'This is not about a man beating up a woman during sex!' he declares. 'Ok, in the following volume they do pick up the S&M bit, but only when she wants,' he says. 'It's the woman allowing the man to play. Then someone from his past shows up and tries to alter the course of events,' Sunil goes on to explain.

The fact of being able to speak so freely about this sexual topic at a party in conservative Chennai feels like proof that something has changed from, say 2008, when I first landed in Bangalore.

A young Indian woman writer I know used a pseudonym on her first erotic novel, only four years ago. But now she decided to go public and own it. She, and a whole nation of women, are finding the courage to talk more openly about sex, in a nation where the artistic expression of eroticism is a most traditional Indian thing (think Khajuraho sculptures and Kamasutra tales and illustrations).

Let's not fool ourselves, while the Indian city may be transforming socially, it's not doing so politically.

A slight impertinence is now allowed, after decades of sullen socialism in which you had to, out of respect or opportunism, camouflage your own privileges and keep them as private as possible.

To be outspoken about sexuality seems to be a new upper middle class privilege.

For example: a couple has invited my wife and I to a Saint Valentine's party called 'Fifty shades of red'.

'Please join us for cocktails & dinner & raise a toast to: the launch of the movie *50 Shades of Grey*, Chinese New Year, our new home, Saint Valentine's day', and the more the merrier, the invite reads.

Didn't make it to the party, but later I saw plenty of photos on Facebook of the customary whiskey fuelled ruby cheeks with everyone laughing in front of red posters with stylized handcuffs. And I wondered if, to be able to joke about this in Modi's fundamentalist India is how 'new Indians' celebrate the Zeitgeist.

Aside from the fact that Tamil Nadu is quite a different context from the Hindustan dreamt by Modi, for these 30-somethings who have graduated from the best Western universities, the new *Modist* India also means gaining a more defined international image.

It is a generation fatigued by the Gandhian iconography of the benign welfare state, the stereotype of Indians as non-violent and submissive, with their good-natured bobbing heads.

Good riddance to the 'Hollywood Party' archetype that Peter Sellers ingrained in the world's imagination. Bye bye birdie num num! Buzz off, Apu!

This is an India that wants to be cool, and is actually making it.

*

Discussing retail masochism for housewives freely is an efficient way to feel modern and contemporary in your own home, even in a Tamil Nadu where a large part of the population, out there in the streets and villages, still wears the most stunning saris while men proudly show their legs peeking out from their lungis.

This, at Dirty Harri's party, is not the India tourists like so much.

It's what I've nicknamed India-Fabindia.

Everyone knows what Fabindia is, a franchise of kurtas, shirts, and furniture, a high-level clothing Ikea you can find even in Rome, Italy. Fabindia culture has even survived the 2008 crisis and keeps communicating a message of modernity born at its foundation—adapting the traditional look and sartorial style to contemporary needs.

Traditional, but new. Sounds contradictory? Get used to it, it's India.

At that very same table at the Park Hyatt, I get drawn into a conversation with Chetan, another shining example of the India-Fabindia category.

He's a young entrepreneur in the hi-fi and photography sector. He travels to Italy more often than I do and knows some Lombard or Tuscan provinces much better than me.

In our house at the beach, I tell him, the raucous fishing boats wake us up at 4 in the morning with their open mufflers ripping like rude jackhammers into the crack of dawn. Hard not to bolt upright in bed.

So he suggests I immediately install a triple layer of glass windows and air conditioning.

'The noise will disappear in a flash,' he assures me, full of enthusiasm.

I ask him, aside from the high cost of this, what would happen then, to the poetry of living on a beach on the Bay of Bengal, if we were to seal our internal reality from the external one in such a way.

He looks at me for a second, understanding our profound differences, and explodes in a smile: 'Ah, well, yes, the poetry in that case would be totally fucked!' And he roars into laughter, changing the subject.

This is the new India-Fabindia of the 50 shades of red.

The India where a pumped up, handsome Sid, sitting to my right, tells me that every weekend he goes pedal to the metal running circles at the Formula 3 circuit of the Madras Motor Sport Club.

The India-Fabindia where Andy walks down from his apartment every morning to play tennis on the swish courts of the Madras Club, before heading to work at his bank.

Where the wiry Hichem wakes up at 4:30 every morning to go horseback riding, and where Divya flies back to, whenever she can leave behind her marketing job in London, once she gets tired of swiping right her somewhat mechanical Tinder dates plucked from a cosmopolitan crowd.

It is also the India of those convinced of being where they are because they deserve it and that those who are below them economically might be there because they are simply lazier, inclined towards vices like cheap moonshine, or are just too ignorant without ambitions or generally incompetent at most things.

Speaking about the poor is so 2017! Although everyone's got an NGO tucked somewhere and ends up having some connections with charity work, either because they feel it's the proper thing to do, or because it kinda looks good on the resume.

An India of privilege? Also.

But this is the India prevalent in the collective imagination, the one displayed on TV or belonging to that Bollywood where the protagonists are wealthy and successful folks—the live bait for the masses of 200 million people surviving below miserable poverty levels, those who get by in true indigence, going to sleep starved of food, and dreams. B-b-bh-oringgg!

Contrary to the Western stereotypical gaze on India, the way Not-So-New India looks at itself is not by obsessing about humanitarian disasters, dowry-wives burnt alive in the kitchens, farmer suicides (which some guru says are caused by 'a lack of spirituality'), or suicide used as blackmail on factory owners in union negotiations.

Let me explain this last one: according to an Indian law, if a rejected lover or a former employee commits suicide leaving behind a farewell note pointing out the person psychologically responsible for this, then the culprit gets arrested, tried and at times convicted.

Suicide can become a posthumous tool of revenge for a single individual, but can also become a lever of collective blackmail from a group of interests, like a workers' cooperative.

The son of a wealthy factory owner told me his father had been threatened by a union: 'If you don't give us what we ask for, one of us will kill himself and leave a signed note saying he did it because of your cruel stinginess.'

The existence of these 'kamikazes of poverty' is one more sign of the further social estrangement among the classes.

But the overgrown boys and girls at Dirty Harry's party cannot be asked to feel constant guilt towards the poverty surrounding them, which anyway, in Tamil Nadu, is nowhere close to what can be witnessed in some northern states.

To succumb to continuous pity, today, is perceived as asking for your own ruin. It's the 'Looking Away' syndrome, also the title of a book by Harsh Mander about 'inequality, prejudice and indifference in New India'.

It's the same India that American intellectual Noam Chomsky describes like this: 'What is really striking to me is the indifference of privileged sectors to the misery of others. You walk through Delhi and cannot miss it but people just don't seem to see it: they put themselves in a bubble and then they don't see it.'

It's the India that considers servants and helpers as cameos of our lives, walking into the set of our daily movie to play small, relevant parts, and then walking off quickly as my friend, the acute novelist Kiran Nagarkar, once remarked.

It is the Party of the Indifferent. Every little conquest of privilege is to be defended with a healthy offhand attitude, which can be justified by the non-attachment of Vedic tradition, conveniently forgetting the equally holy Vedic compassion.

How does this affect those who haven't grown up here?

How do you cope with the beggars, for example, if you haven't grown up around Indian beggars who are quite a different category from the mendicants of Europe?

I personally reached into Italian literature for help, to unearth what I've nicknamed 'The Manganelli Technique'. Not the most humanitarian, but efficient.

In his fascinating *Experiment with India*, Italian writer Giorgio Manganelli expanded on his technique used to deal with beggars on the streets of Bombay in 1975. He describes being followed for half an hour by a little boy, one evening, and how, at first, the writer tried to avoid him. Wrong.

'By switching lanes to elude him, I made him understand that I was uncomfortable, and thus it was worth insisting with me. Because the Westerner not only feels pity, not only is sensitive to the signs of disease, but he's sufficiently lascivious to know the preclusions of disgust, and also to be inclined towards feelings of guilt.'

Manganelli diagnosed how his guilt feelings were being cheekily manipulated and decided to seek the help of his interpretation of Indian philosophy: 'I understood instantly that in such society, in such culture, there's no room for individual pity, there's none of that painful, desperate charity that ties the West to the naturally dying—nor does the beggar, the misfortunate feel pity for himself.'

Far fetched, but it leads to a technique: 'I resolved not to give any charity, not just to satisfy my innate avarice, but also to see if it would be possible to accept misery, disease and misfortune as an event that, differently placed, had another meaning than in our world.'

So Manganelli goes native: 'It is an ascetic exercise. From the moment he starts with his whining sing-a-song he must be declared non-existent. And thus you have to speed up your stride, not look at him, or if you look towards him you must soar your gaze above him or right through him. You never attempt to cross the street abruptly, unless you're almost being run over by a car. You stop, you let the beggar repeat until you feel nauseous at his story. You never answer to his insistent question: "What country are you from?" Because, since he doesn't exist, it is forbidden for him to ask questions. If you communicate to him, not with gestures, but with the entire body, with your own stillness, that he "does not exist"—which in a way he already knows—he's persuaded. His sing-a-song gets tired, he gets distracted, he eyes another pale face and abruptly abandons the indifferent to pick up again his lament elsewhere.'

However surgically cold and insensitive this lesson may appear, it captures the essence of what is known in India as the 'Looking Away Syndrome' which allows everyone to co-habit with probably the biggest inequalities you'll ever see in this world.

Yes, India tests you.

I've also arrived here full of my 360 degree compassion, full of pain for the poor, the beggars and, yes, the lepers. A bit of a Dominique Lapierre's *City of Joy* parody.

This constant alertness towards the raucous jazz improvisation that is the Indian Street was drawing in my attention so intensely that I felt energized and drained at the same time.

Although I've never been known for my arithmetic skills, it didn't take me long to figure that if I started to give rupees left and right, soon enough I'd be in the same predicament as the crowd with the extending hand.

Inhuman? This sacred apathy also affects wealthy foreigners who move here for a long period, the so-called 'expats' or rich migrants.

*

Speaking to my mother-in-law, I was told of an important shift emerging within this community. While until 20 years ago diplomats, executives and managers sent to India from Europe, Asia, Australia or the US felt a duty to participate actively with donations and time devoted to associations of volunteers, religious or secular, the new generations of expats seem much more immune from temptation towards charitable activities.

It is as if these Westerners, Koreans or Japanese *nouveau riche* (hey, better *nouveau riche* that not *riche* at all, as Imelda Marcos once famously said) have already migrated here with a human aridity caused by having to survive their own economic crisis—so much so that they don't feel a duty to collectively succour 'the poor Indians.'

They ask themselves this: if India has the funds to send 104 satellites into space and enough money to invest in atomic weapons or to send a couple of supersonic BrahMos Cruise missiles at Mach 3 speed for 400 km in the sky, why should foreigners be burdened with the cost of helping the Indian downtrodden?

Previously, when expats often hailed from decadent noble or old-money families, there was maybe a sense of guilt or moral duty, corroborated at times by a socialist equalizing dictum or a Christian calling.

These new expats, children of the Third Way, a mixture of free market liberalism and a limited welfare state, are more often than not survivors themselves; self-made people arriving from a more modernized West with maybe less nepotism and familism. (I underline that 'maybe' twice.)

As the popular Roman saying goes: 'Talk to the impoverished rich man, but keep away from the rich who was poor.'

*

I ran into an American older lady once who'd been living in India for decades and she had a good word of advice for any expat. 'If you live in India long enough, one day you will be lining up somewhere at a bank counter, a post office or at a government desk. And, all of a sudden, you'll see this white person who will totally lose it and scream at the top of their lungs in rage and impatience. And that screaming white person will be you.'

Recently, during those testing demonetization days, I actually did find myself at a post office with only one person queuing up behind me. Well, beside me, truly.

I felt this middle-age man's belly button, cushioned by a healthy rice-nurtured pillow of fat, rub impatiently and sweatily against my elbow. I considered turning around and explaining the concept of 'at arm's length'—I sensed maybe my time to burst out like that American lady had prophesied had come.

For some arcane reason, I contained myself.

I wanted to go Indian. To have patience, to accept a different relationship to privacy and body space.

I calmed down, the corners of my mouth placidly curled up while my eyelids dropped a fraction of an inch into a placid gaze.

It turned out the cashier did not have change for my bank note. No change, blame it on demonetization. An instant of tension arose at the prospect of not being able to send my urgent letter, but the sensation didn't have time to flourish. The pot-bellied man immediately spread open his wallet and volunteered to dish out the 20 extra rupees I needed to send the letter. Out of his good heart or out of the need to speed up the process, it doesn't matter.

Somehow my being patient, in an Indian way, I'd dare to say, had served me better than being that white person who loses his wits.

Ageing in India: that shift from stud to uncle, from hottie to aunty

Or girls gotta get laid and sooner or later they gotta get married

'He died right in my arms, man!'

Harri is still shocked as he tells me what just happened to him. It's a week after his birthday party. Having gone underground to cure his dinosaur hangover, he's now back in business.

We're riding in the backseat of his car, up the ECR, on our way to a party at some friends' posh new house.

'Yes, he died in my arms. We were at the Madras Cricket Club. Talking, just like you and me now. He had just turned 48. He sat down at the bar next to me. He said, "I've done 11 km on the treadmill." And then, "I'm not feeling so good." That's when he fell down. I got in the ambulance with him. He was going, man. But at the hospital, we thought he was going to make it. No, dude. By the time his wife reached the hospital, he was done. I had to tell her.

'Shit, man! Life is like *Game of Thrones*, you know? This is how things are with people. The guy who thinks he's going to become the king gets beheaded. Good guy gets it when it's least expected in the plot. He died in my arms, basically. Shit yeah, I'm shocked. It's a test of emotional strength for me, some friends said. Yeah, right. But how strong should I become? I don't want to be strong. I want to party on, dude. And why should I become so strong, so I can become a wailing wall for people who just like to talk about their problems and make them your problems without ever listening to my advice? Why?'

Harri is on a roll. He's about the same age as the friend who just died. The Danger Zone, between 48 and 52, when you are statistically most likely to die of a heart attack.

A bitter antipasto of a death-thought which might then disappear for a while, as you get a second wind. But it will show up again later in life, when you're older. When you go from stud to uncle, from hottie to aunty.

Harri is youthful, full of strength and drive. Still unmarried. And has no problems finding a girlfriend. Yet, he dishes out advice to the single lady friends who've entered their own danger zone, which you cross once you're older than 23 years and still unmarried in India.

'These two girls I know just had a horrible fight while on vacation in Coonoor, man. One of them was eyeing this guy. So she went to get him a drink. When she came back, her friend was in the thick of conversation with the target man. "You've done it again, haven't you!" the generous drink-getter yells at the boy-snatcher. Growl, cat fight! Happens all the time. Girls gotta get laid. And sooner rather than later they gotta get married, man!'

Harri laughs with his booming joy-thunder.

A few years ago in Rome, I picked up another wise saying. At first it made me laugh but it proves to be true in many modern cities around the world. In the ancient metropolis, women giving advice to friends who are about to ditch their boyfriend or husband often say to each other: 'If you throw your man out the window at the fourth floor, by the time he falls to the third floor another woman has already caught him.'

Harri's advice? 'To these girls on a lookout for a man I say: stop seeking, polish yourself, get better, the world will come for you, someone will come and take a bite! Just take it easy. Stop dwelling on carcasses, stop liking bad energy, people! But, hey, I'm not fucking Fleetwood Mac, so I've gotta think of my own life, right?'

Right, Harri the Hurricane. Dirty Harri. Harri Harri Krishna. He does talk tough, but always shows up when needed. He can't help it. Big heart.

This is friendship in southern India in the 21st Century, among the upper middle class, those who can afford a house and a driver, who are set on a job, who are climbing up, always hoping to reach a step higher.

This is also the driving force for people like my brilliant, loving friend Michael, the son of a house cook who got a job in a call centre and then became a successful, world-travelling PR man for a major international bank. No caste constraints could keep this guy down. Sends egalitarian love shivers up and down your fore-arm skin, goose-bumping away with meritocratic pride.

Everyone wants to improve, get a bigger slice of the pie. So many compromises are made along the way. Even in the well-off upper middle class of urban India.

Girls still get married to violent husbands surrounded by the silent acquiescence of all friends. 'It's her business,' they say, cloaking their fear under the excuse of granting privacy.

'She knew what she was getting into...'

As long as the husband provides a luxury car, spa breaks, plastic surgery abroad, it's all actually ok, it's 'their own private business'.

None of the enlightened, contemporary self-proclaimed feminist women of Chennai's *haute bourgeoisie* engage actively in putting a stop to it. They may gossip about it, though.

The ones who rant and rave on social media against Indian men, against the lewd pigs, they say nothing. No one I know challenges the violent husband for what he actually is—that mummy-spoiled brute, taking advantage of these specific dredges of macho history, still surviving here, as they survive in Italy and in many other parts of the world.

This is not what makes the news, no burning spouse in the kitchen, no beheading, but the constant humiliation of the banality of the middle-class' domestic abuse of power.

So it's all ok, the bruises are not a public crime, it's something she's ok with. 'It feeds into their sex life,' the gossipers say. 'They make up in bed,' they snicker.

And when the libido goes, what's left is the money or, at least, some prestige from the husband's kin.

I know very well the dynamics. I grew up in a very similar family and that is why I notice and probably why I have a hard time ignoring this.

But in the care-free, happy-go-lucky scene of Chennai's upper middle class, all this is dust under the carpet and you won't notice a thing at a house party with some delicious Mexican tacos and condensed milk-based lime cake.

In fact, after our car ride, Harri and I are finally walking into Chetan and Priyanka's house for a little get together, in the heart of Chennai, not too far from the Madras Club. Beers and cocktails flow freely, while that innocent soft rock revisitation of '80s hits called nu-disco plays in the perfect sound system.

People gather on the Bauhaus-style cement terrace to smoke and chat. Anaka is a successful fashion designer frustrated about the music mix. She's in her early 30s; luscious curves, full lips and all, framed by a leonine mane of curly hair dancing around her luminous smile which often ends in thumping, contagious laughter. She's been back from the States a few years now and she's still not found anyone who's into hip hop as much as I am.

So she's excited that I play a song by Young Thug on the Sonos sound system. But it's got a bit of rough lyrics about 'bitches and hoes', that sort of stupid pre-Harvey Weinstein, Roman Polanski, Bill Cosby scandals thing.

'This is what feeds masculine oppression!' the lady of the house says as she hits the stop button. Priyanka, Chetan's attractive, vibrant Florida-born wife, has the standard Indian classic charm mixed with teenager spirit. She's a fun and wild millennial with an Instagram, blogger bent that will tell you to 'Eat local!' and shamelessly insta-story away the entire day of her two rowdy children.

'This? Hip hop is masculine oppression?' old, out-of-touch me asks.

'Yes, *this* hip-hop is exactly that,' I get femalesplained as Priya shoves me out of her sound system and spins Iggy Azalea's 'Pu$$y', a female view of talking about her own genitalia, vagina, vulva and clitoris and what men should do to them.

Girrrrlll powerrrr.

In the comfort of your sound system.

Not in reality.

In Chennai's reality, it's all still pretty much uphill, let's face it, ladies. Emotions have to be hidden. This is true in general of most Chennaites I've met, which sets them clearly apart from their Mumbai, Delhi and Kolkata counterparts.

What is it about Chennai folks that make them so famously bashful about showing their emotions and passion? Is it the Tam Bram (Tamil Brahmin) curse? Or is that a blessing? This may explain why they allow it to tackily blossom in almost every Kollywood flick. It's called artistic sublimation of a repressed emotion.

Paging Doctor Freud!

All that Vedic wisdom, calming those desires, who some think make our life worth living, might lead into an overly sedated existence and a youth that can't get into hip hop, as Anaka complains.

This is a juncture this India seems to be facing now: stick to the bh-horing yet shaky harmony of tradition or indulge the double-edged excitement of contemporary fun?

Allegedly, the passion runs wild with the emotionally freer Dalit, where the party's at, but stays buttoned up in a Prussian self-controlled life cloaked in rasgulla sweets, hidden by the supposedly sattvic silent smiles of the upper classes, who know better than letting emotions run free into disorderly chaos! And who know how to shut up about what really happens behind closed doors.

This is so reminiscent of the Catholic bigoted reality I grew up with in a provincial town near Venice—it's astounding I find myself in it again, after a long escape through cosmopolitan capitals around the world.

*

You have to understand one thing about Indian terminology—tradition and family are so central to culture here, that everyone is either your uncle, aunt, cousin or your bro. Cousins abound naturally, whereas brotherly love is often announced, though not necessarily always practiced.

'Uncle' is anyone who is older then you, old enough to be seen from across a generation gap, however short a distance that may be, here in India. It's when you stop being a young man.

There comes a phase in the life of a male in India when if you wear a t-shirt you still might be addressed as 'Hey, dude', but if you wear a formal, ironed shirt, or even that rare tie, then it'll immediately be 'Hello, uncle!'

And aunties, well, aunties are a stage in a woman's life. It's a delicate issue…How can I put it? It's when youthful vigour may begin to dwindle, substituted by a wisdom which can be played out in many ways: from the charmingly warm to the annoyingly sanctimonious, since aunties sometimes do tend to become the arms and brains of the Moral Brigades.

Some Chennai aunties can be the epitome of this. Chennai aunties may very well be the sturdy guards empowered with the task to guard the palace of temperance and balance. Aunties who were hotties...

In fact, whenever I find myself in the company of millennial hotties and studs, like these friends gathered at Chetan and Priyanka's party, from the out-of-place observation point of a 50-something vellai intruder by marriage, I can't help noticing the auntie concealed within the hottie, or the uncle hidden in the stud, waiting to blossom as years go by.

I then engage in the solipsistic game of mentally noting down the tic, the banality or the wisdom of the uncle creeping through the vigour of fading youth. Or I hear the increasingly nasal tone of the hotties, slowly shape-shifting into the aunties they will soon become.

By reverse, I savour the remnant signs of stud-nature in an 80-year-old uncle who still has a wild streak in him, be it intellectual or physical, driving wildly in traffic, having that original, against-the-grain thought. And I love observing the charming seduction of the hottie which is still hiding within the auntie; the sensual beauty that never left the gaze, the languid movement of the shoulder while fixing the sari shawl and flicking away a fallen white hair.

I literally run into troves of such aunties almost every morning on my health walk at dawn with my beloved, smiling father-in-law.

They wear sneakers and saris.

They are not jogging and they are not really walking. They're kind of strolling, really, aren't they?

I would call it spiritual strolling, to be precise.

I get it that this is what the atmosphere and mandate of the Theosophical Society is supposed to inspire. And yet I know they are not doing it just so they can repeat mantras, which some chant out loud, sometimes in a heavenly hum.

Aunties draped in saris, overweight, languid, calm. Too calm, really. Bordering on the soporiferous, honestly.

How many times I've witnessed this scene, in Chennai—the lady of some charity NGO walks to the podium with a prepared speech she hasn't rehearsed enough.

'It is suuuch a pleasure to be here...' she drones on interminably, her vacuous speech intended to evoke great feelings of Gandhian humanity and warmth often lasts longer than the performance or book talk we're actually there to witness.

Don't they see their uncle-husbands and uncle-friends nodding off to sleep in the audience? Probably not. Or they do, but who cares, right?

What am I doing here? It was intriguing in the beginning. Now I begin to understand the frustration of younger people in the crowd. It's a slower speed aunties are on. This ritual is empty, rehashed. 'And now it is with great pleasure...' The pleasure is all yours, really.

Aunties are everywhere. Aunties have the power. Aunties, what would we do without you? Aunties, you move the social world, you prod it on. Aunties are all the Mother Goddess, in a way.

Aunties show up at the Condé Nast event, aunties are at the Crown Plaza benefit theatre show. At the Madras Book Club launch. They are the majority.

As much as Chennai youth likes to bitch about aunties, if it weren't for them, there might be no cultural life at all. Aunties are coming out of the woods, they are taking charge of the table; they're elbowing their way into the buffet.

Nothing's gonna stop them now!

They are the guardians of tradition. And there's something to be said in recognition of the important role of aunties' culture.

Aunties are the mothers of the very same people who frequent the Formula 3 circuit, the tennis tournament, the horse stables, the golf course, the cliquish post-colonial clubs, the parties at the 5-star hotels where alcohol can be served.

They are the ones who, within the glands of family metabolism, control that very important vein of culture called tradition.

The new battling the old, conservation vs innovation, status quo vs new.

Aunty-culturalists…Aunty culture makes sure that

tradition stays as a healthy anchor to avoid the pitfalls of transformation. While at the same time slowly blocking a possibly healthy progress.

It is the reins fastened on the mouth of the horse of time, facing the challenge of dosing the right amounts of tradition and rigour with the oxygen of change.

LATIN LOVERS, HATERS AND VOLUNTOURISTS: 50 SHADES OF WHITEYS IN INDIA

Pros and cons of being an Italian in Tamil Nadu, discovering the well-integrated, trendy-society and the wild party-techno whiteys and, yes, grumpy me. Being a volun-tourist with Mother Teresa's nuns, infiltrating a case study in culture shock on Facebook and hearing an uncomfortable revelation from Dirty Harri.

A Venetian in Madras

On being a whitey in a changing India

> There once was a man from Madras
> Whose balls were made of brass
> In stormy weather
> They clanged together
> 'till sparks flew out of his arse!
> —Adult Limerick

I'm out of breath. Sweating.

Minuscule sea shells crackling under my bare feet, as I run from a ship wreck, dogs at my heels.

High tide waves keep crashing on the steep shore. Up ahead, a group of Tamil men crowding the way.

I wipe my forehead with the back of my wrist.

Seven o'clock and it's already hot.

It's been a damp 15 minutes' morning jog, so far. I reach the turn-around point—the remains of a fishing boat—and now I must endure another 15 in order to complete my daily distance goal, dictated by the manipulating app flashing on the smartphone in my pocket.

To my right, I catch a glimpse of a guy pointing his phone camera at me and clicking away.

I lower the visor of my torn military green cap and turn the other way. That's when he starts jogging by my side, even though he's wearing long trousers, a long sleeve shirt and flip flops.

In Italian *fare l'Indiano*, to act like an Indian means to feign total indifference. Just like a fakir ignores the pointy nails under his butt. Think Manganelli technique.

So I 'act like an Indian', *faccio l'indiano*, and pretend there's no six foot tall stranger suddenly jogging by my side.

'Are you from the US?' he asks, straight-faced.

'What?!' I blurt out, not sure I heard right.

'Are you from the US?' he repeats jogging alongside me.

'What?! No. Leave me alone.'

'Are you from the US?' Now he whips out his camera again and prepares to take a close-up. Again, I turn my chin towards the Bay of Bengal as I try to speed up.

'No photos, man! Tourist ille! I'm not a tourist. I live here. Leave me the heck alone, dude!'

I attempt to lose him, but I'm a bit out of breath.

He sprints ahead, maybe just to prove he can run faster than 'the guy from the US'. Or to make me pay for my rudeness.

I buckle for trouble, but now it is this improvised paparazzo who runs out of steam. The sprint got the best of his lungs. He slows down.

I pass him again, Buggy, Bagheera, Zelda following closely behind. Now he drags his feet to join a group waiting for him to return from his morning defecation in the wilds.

Being a whitey in Tamil Nadu has more pros than cons. But it does have some minor cons.

Once my Mars-red Ecosport was running out of gas, as I was driving alone down the ECR highway, so I stopped at a station, turned off the engine, waited for assistance. As I turned around, I saw a boy staring with his jaw dropped, nostrils dilated, eyes wide open.

'Hey, hey,' he elbowed his colleague at the pump station in this lost stretch of road, south of Mamallapuram.

'Look, look!' he seemed to be saying, while pointing at me.

What? Look at what, man?! I thought.

Look at that vellai! Driving! Alone! In a car! That's what. Simple as that. What else could it be?

I checked if I had something on my nose or food on my beard. Nothing.

I was the joke. The thing out of place. Which is how I've always felt about myself anyway, so why the annoyance?

It was the entire *me* who was surprising to the boys. Nothing menacing, yet still a form of reverse discrimination. The kind, in this case, that is mostly advantageous to the revered and respected victim, of course. But still…nothing wrong in being an amusing little white puppet in a red car. And yet…

And yet, here I am, a whitey victim of whitey mythology. It was the colonialist culture which has ingrained this sense of difference mixed with deference, cloaked in respect, so I can't complain that I find myself on the receiving end of this. Yes, a whitey victims of our own whitey mythologies.

*

I know what it feels like to see a white face after months and months in Tamil Nadu. It happens to me too. That's part of being a mappillai vellai.

After months of living in a part of India that is not yet ruined by the plague of tourism, after months on end of seeing mostly Tamil people, Tamil smiles on Tamil faces, when you do finally spot the occasional pale, waxy-skinned Australian, German, or British tourist attempting to blend in by wearing a hippy tie dye, bangles and necklaces, dreadlocks or braids or simply wearing the comfortable uniform of the Patagonia international army, the mosquito-repelling baggy trousers, the pink, clip-on fanny packs, men with pony-tails and capri pants, or hiding under the wide brimmed jungle-style Crocodile Dundee hats in downtown Chennai, you think: *oh, look, look, whiteys!*

And you stare. I mean, I do. I was one of them.

When I first came to India in 2008, I resolved to never get caught by all that poisoned water I was sure was everywhere in India. Not me!

I was going to be prepared. I was not going to die of dehydration in the dangerous jungles in mysterious India.

I would lean down by the murky creek and stick my little glass straws connected to my newly purchased portable purifier and ha-ha! I would drink myself back to strength, making it safely out, *Shantaram!* from that bacterial hell hole, damn it!

Of course, I never once used the expensive contraption. Never found any use for it, since, obviously, bottled water is available pretty much everywhere, as testified by the plastic debris blanket which reassuringly plasters Mother India in just about every corner.

Yes, I was that diffident, scared white man tentatively inching through the constant threats of In-di-aaaah.

'Oooo, I'd love to go to In-di-aaah, but I'm so scarrrred...'

How often do I hear this phrase in Italy?

Compared to the Tamil languor and apparent sweetness hiding behind the smooth skin and the *santosha* post-prandial gaze of most locals, whiteys look just so stressed, consumed, wrinkly, tense, pursed-lipped, nervous and fidgety.

When I see them (us), I perceive finally what I must look like to the Tamil eye: crazy, stressed, rude, tense, out of sync with the flow, bro.

Not a pretty sight. I realize it sounds like the thought

of someone gone native, but to me it's a reminder of what an overly determined power of the will can do to our physiognomies—proof of what weather and mentality can do in altering the external aspect of your body.

It's harsh and difficult to live in this South Indian equatorial climate. It's tough for everyone to face the economic conditions here, the Chennai traffic, the corruption, the abuses of power, caste and class, politics and discrimination.

And yet it's all so well hidden, in Tamil Nadu, so skilfully repressed by the wide-spread customs and mores.

But the vellais, the goras, dragging their over-heated, swollen white feet into town, they show their strife.

The lines of their stories are etched in the wood of their skin.

As the late Italian actor Anna Magnani once said: 'Please don't retouch my wrinkles. It took me so long to earn them.'

Our faces are truly open books, telling stories of cold winters full of flus and colds, taxes that are too high, traffic too thick, and aggressive attitudes with each other, while that November freezing cold settles into the continent of Europe and makes everyone's soul cringe.

I do know what I look like to the eyes of these two Tamil boys waiting to fill up my tank.

Odd, out of place, curious, exotic.

In Tamil Nadu in the 21st century, my gas station episode mirrors somewhat what it must've been like to see my Gujarati father-in-law wearing bell-bottom pants, a tight elegant shirt, curls down to his shoulder while hitchhiking alone from Venice to Naples, on his 1966 Italian journey.

A handsome, Jain vegetarian Gujju from Madras loving the land of pizza and pasta. And being loved back by an economically booming Italy, where wealth was much more equally distributed than today.

When I took him and the whole acquired family for a tour of Italy after our wedding in 2014, I warned him that the country I grew up in had radically changed since his last trip here. Italy is not as kind towards the browner race as it was in 1966.

Increasing waves of migration from Asia and Africa have brought out the old fascist and racist spirit in the land of pizza/pasta.

Turns out he again got by splendidly with the locals, maybe thanks to his smile and serene disposition. Still a cool cat after all these years.

'E i marò?'

In Italy, Indians are not as loved as they used to be by many right-wing imbeciles, after two Italian marines were detained under house arrest in Delhi for a very long period, suspected of killing two Kerala fishermen in the high seas. The Italian sharp-shooters said they mistook the fishermen victims for pirates assaulting their oil tanker.

An Indian who lives in Italy, after reading an article I'd published about reactions I get as an Italian in India, tweeted this to me:

@carlopizzati top responses I get as an Indian in Italy:

1 Kabir Bedi

2 ooh I always wanted to go to India/do you do yoga

3 Send us our Marò.

Let me explain.

Point no. 1: actor and all around wonderful guy Kabir Bedi played a courageous, egalitarian Malaysian pirate in a majorly successful TV series in the '70s. Wherever he shows up in Italy he's still greeted by 40- to 50-somethings who sing to the top of their lungs the refrain of the opening credits song of *Sandokan*, an Italian six-part television series based upon the novels of Emilio Salgari, 'Sandokan! Sandokan! *Lenta sale la marea...*' He achieved more with that TV hit, than 70 years of diplomatic relationships between the two countries.

Point no. 2: By now you should know all about the Western stressed mind going to India to do yoga, the dream of yoga-people.

Point no. 3: It hasn't been as easy to be an Indian in

Italy since two Italian marines known as '*i marò*' were arrested off the coasts of India in February 2012.

Some people in Italy have been up in arms about this. Faded, starchy sheets have been hanging for years outside some city halls pleading to 'Bring back our marines!'

Two protestors walked 280 km to bring a letter to the Vatican, ask for divine intervention. A member of Parliament posed for photographers while inserting two miniature statuettes of the marines in a Christmas nativity scene. Another right-wing politician promised he'd steal the flag from the Indian embassy and cause a diplomatic incident. He didn't deliver.

Chest thumping antics were accompanied by Internet racist trolls foaming at the mouth against 'those dirty Indians!' 'those primordial types!' and much worse.

Rap songs were recorded accusing the Italian government of not doing enough; Miss India-Italy beauty pageants indefinitely suspended; permissions not granted to shoot a Bollywood film in Lecco.

The mayor of a town in the North tried to force Indian residents to sign a letter condemning the Indian government and asking for the release of the marò.

Indian chaat stands almost got kicked out of a street food fair; there was a failed attempt to launch a 'Boycott Indian Products' campaign, and the mayor of the town of Fasano, in Puglia, formally rejected the invitation to attend an Agarwal and Mehta wedding, which would have brought 10 million euros to his local economy.

A very tough chapter in personal, diplomatic and economic relations between the two 'I' countries, which today seems to be drifting away.

Italians in India still have it easy

'What country are you from?' asks the cheerful cashier at the corner food store selling pasta and fancy foreign food in Kalakshetra colony.

'Italy.'

'Best in the heart! Excellent country,' he explains, hitting his chest. And then he qualifies his enthusiasm with what I've come to christen the 'pizza masala mantra': 'Aah, Italy…ferrari-lamborghini-soniagandhi-berlusconi-bunga bungaaaa!'

Let the record show that the Sonia Gandhi bit was whipped out more often and more cheerfully before the 2014 elections that brought Mr Narendra Modi and the BJP to power.

After that, only a 30 per cent tranche of Indians I meet seem to be impressed when I specify that Sonia Maino was actually born 20 km from my hometown of Valdagno.

The fact is that before being Italian I'm a Venetian, having grown up a 45-minute commute ride away from Rome, Venice. So I try to specify that to the inquiring Indian minds who are widely overcome by the pressing need to know: 'What country are you from?'

I know my first predecessors here in Tamil Nadu might have been Roman traders, setting up camp in Ariyankuppam, south of Pondicherry, leaving a trail of coins and pottery that are still being dug up an hour south from where I live now.

And I know that the Venetian messer Marco Polo also came through these lands, on his way back from his famous Chinese residency.

I also know that later, in 1656, another Venetian set up camp in Madras. Dottor Niccolò Manucci lived here until 1711 and then moved to Pondicherry for the last five years of a very rich life, after the death of his wife Elizabeth Clark, described in historical accounts as an Anglo-mestizo, which my Gujarati-Welsh wife prefers to define as 'the hybrid model'. A Venetian in Madras married to a hybrid model—history *is* cyclical.

So, I am conscious of the tradition, of the nothing new under the sun, in these exotic coasts of an Indian State most Europeans have a hard time placing on the map. Tamil what?

And yet, even though us Venetians have been coming and setting up residency for centuries, if you get spotted alone at the wheel of a car, it's still elbow-on-the-ribs and hey, look, look at that vellai!

Or, 'Here comes that guy, what's his name? Tishani's husband, c'mon.'

Or, 'Wait!...Marco. No, no...Paolo...hmm...'

I'm happy to be sidelined as Mr Doshi—the husband of the published poet and contemporary dancer with an international following.

Even when I go for the second time to have a bespoke suite made at Gatsby's, down the ECR, the owner I call 'refined Rafiq' has a hard time remembering who I am.

Basically, if I had a lower profile I'd be dead.

As I leave the fitting room he asks:

'So, how long have you been here in Chennai?'

'Er...a long time, Rafiq. I've had a shirt and a suit made here. With you...remember? I stop by at least once every two weeks to shop in your store, buy food from you, eat in your restaurant.'

Silence and embarrassment. But, I mean, how hard is it to fix in your memory an Italian who has Pizza in his last name. Come on. Pizza and tea, can't get more Italian-Indian than that. Pizzati. That nondescript Italian guy, with the nondescript haircut and stubble, the nondescript hairstyle, but that memorable Pizza last name. No? No.

'You even told me about your vacation in Mexico, how you liked Mexican people and felt they were closer to Indians in their view of the world and life...'

Empty gaze. There I am, making myself invisible in Madras, like the first night I was here.

'Ah, yes...' he pretends.

'I'm Tishani's husband...? Carlo?'

'Oh, yeees…of cooourse!' Deep smile of relief.

'I mean, I know all vellais look alike,' I say, 'but still…'

'No, yes, sorry, no, yes, of course. I know, I know, yes, now I remember. Sorry. It's just that I'm used to seeing you with Tishani so…'

'Yes, well, I'm ok if you want to call me Mr Doshi, really. I don't have an ego problem. I mean, not any longer. I mean, not as much. But, yes, you can go with "Mr Doshi" if you prefer, really.'

I try to flash out my Tamil smile with the slowest, most imperceptible head bob I can muster, so that it doesn't feel like I'm mocking the locals.

As a consolation, a mortified Rafiq personally delivers a couple of yummy home-made chocolate candies to my restaurant table where I sit all alone, next door to the men's fashion shop.

'Here, Carlo, please try them and tell me what you think. Hope you like them, Carlo. Please tell me what you think of them, Carlo.'

Later, Refined Rafiq will become my sympathetic Facebook friend. I've hopped over that hurdle. After eight years of knowing each other casually.

I've battled all my life as a shy exhibitionist with this contradictory need to stand out, but at the same time to be invisible.

Hiding was my favourite pastime as a child, in the long, boring afternoons I spent parked away from a wrathful father, stowed away, during closing hours, among the darkened shelves of the antique pharmacy connected to my grandparents' home in the village of humid Recoaro Terme, the closest thing to Gangtok you'll find in Northern Italy.

I'd stick my little hands into huge jars of coloured ginevrine candies and chomp my way into an epidemic of cavities that I had to get painfully filled by the time I was 12. I started very early to learn how to cohabit with pain. A useful skill, much later, in India.

Mostly, I liked to find a corner in the shadow of the closed shop and hide.

From whom? Who knows? Probably from the perusing gaze of a future me who now examines that child who loved to read books and comic book stories of the cowboy Tex Willer battling the evil Mephisto; the dreams of Jules Verne; voyages or Emilio Salgari and his Malaysian pirates like Sandokan; and Phileas Fogg rounding the globe in 80 days; and Kipling and his cartoonish exoticism; Jack London and Cervantes and his hallucinated knight and so on until Gabriel Garcia Márquez and Mario Vargas Llosa and the list never stopped...

Lost in the fantasy of stories, hidden from reality in the spiral nebula of literature, later shifting to the K's of the brothers Karamazov, Kafka, Kurt Vonnegut and on to Bernhard, Handke, Faulkner, Melville and on and on, not knowing I'd soon join a life of adventures in the Americas, North and South, not dissimilar to those I was reading, all to finally land in Tamil Nadu and become Mr Doshi, the husband of the internationally published poet, novelist, contemporary dancer and my marvellous lady, Tishani; and the son-in-law of a wonderful couple of youthful and cheerful hearts.

*

The point is I'm actually a local by marriage. So even though I may appear like one of them foreigners, I have reason to feel more integrated.

I have outlived the early fears followed by the enamourment with the exotic. I have gone through the fascination, visceral passion for this diversity and now I judge it from up close, from the seniority of my 10 years of acquaintance with this India.

I have my ups and downs, as I'd have anywhere else.

Contrary to many other expats, I live in an Indian household. Although it's an 'Anglo-mestizo' one, as old fogeys would call it, this gives me a right to say, at times, things like: 'Chennai sucks!'

I mean, it doesn't really, but I feel I have earned the right to be grumpy about it when I need to, just like a local.

Not like any starry eyed expat who's moved here to finally be who they really are, who found in this context the freedom to be themselves, as they had not really, truly and deeply been able to be elsewhere.

Their happiness here is related to their being external players, never really, truly integrated, no matter how many more parties and dinners they attend.

Being an occasionally grumpy mappillai means I belong, dammit. Just like being truly Italian means complaining about Italy any chance you get.

And although some locals still might not get it, and feel that as a foreigner-whitey I'm presumed to only show admiration and respect for the hosting country, hey, I've got news, I'm rooted enough to have earned the right to speak my mind.

From an Indian perspective, as a bona fide Overseas Citizen of India, not as a judgemental outsider who compares cultures in a dubious hierarchy.

Italians in India, a Facebook study in culture shock

'I just wanna have a drink! No Indians allowed, not even Westernised!'

There are plenty of truly maladjusted foreigners in India.

I find some of them lurking on an online self-help, closed Facebook group called 'Italians in India' that I've belonged to for years as a voyeuristic, silent member.

This useful, generous group is run with the best intentions. You'll find questions and answers by Italian expats wanting to know how to set up their lives in Bangalore for a two-year contract, how to open a bank account in Delhi, get a phone connection in Mumbai.

It's administered by people full of love and enthusiasm for India. But it can also occasionally harbour the frustrated rant of the culture shock victim who, after three years, is still alienated and really should ask to be transferred back to the West.

There are expats who really hate it here, but can't move out or they'll lose the only job they can have at the moment.

Victims. Sad cases.

In his FB photo, Matteo wears mirror shades and has his picture upside down. I don't think it's because he's hiding. It's more because he wants to exude charisma and symptomatic mystery and because he wants to convey what he perceives to be his intriguing rebellious nature. But also because he feels upside down where he lives.

Chandigarh is not the place for him. Nor is India. It emerges clearly from his post that sets off a very revealing discussion:

'Looking for a Westerner in Chandigarh! Please no time-wasters, I just wanna have a drink outdoors! No Indians allowed, not even Westernised!'

All these exclamation marks underline the fact that he's just about had it. He's not alone. Mirco is sympathetic to his cause and replies:

'Can't help you, but I understand you...'

From Chatarpur, Massimiliano has also developed the widely diffused auditory allergy to India, and Indians, as he replies to Matteo:

'I can't stand them anymore, them and their car horns!'

Susanna attempts a soothing, kind, new age/yoga pranayama solution for him:

'Breathe deeply and go into a little corner, then scream until you lose your voice. Sometimes it works [smiley face].'

Daniel is more dramatic, *all'italiana*:

'Or throw something against the wall, that works too.'

Luca hints to a specific problem he has with India:

'Car horns are the least of the evils.'

Massimiliano is not convinced. India brought out the little KKK man hiding inside him, as he admits that:

'I have never been a racist, but after 3 years here…'

Carlo—not me, I promise—tries to lighten up with what he thinks is a funny joke:

'There's a saying I heard from an Italian friend who resides in Namibia: do you know the difference between a tourist and a racist??……5 minutes!!!! I say it as a resident [three winking faces].'

Daniel seals the lid of this telling thread:

'Ahahahah maybe not after 5 minutes, but after a few months it can be. XD.'

Fight, flight and filter. These are the three Fs you are taught to face in intercultural communication classes of Professor Weaver.

When you first get to a foreign culture, you will *fight* the local customs that differ so much from yours.

Then you will want to take *flight*, escape the foreign culture, go back to yours.

And then you will start *filtering* what you see through the pink lenses of your own cultural pre-conceptions.

There is even a W-shaped graph explaining rather scientifically the possible rollercoaster of moods a foreigner may go through when faced with a new, hosting culture, for a year.

Starts off on a high, dips to the lowest point in mid-stay, slowly rises up to euphoria again until it's time to leave and then there's counter-culture shock, back home, again sad and confused, only to slowly inch back to normalcy.

Many of these Facebook commentators are experiencing these three 'Fs', as they're riding the culture shock W-rollercoaster. But they don't know it.

A hard-core course in intercultural communication should be mandatory for inexperienced travellers, before sending them to work abroad, especially in such an intensely culture-specific nation like India.

*

I remember the first shocked and maladjusted Italian I met once in Tranquebar.

This bushy eyebrowed man was living at the same hotel where I was staying. Permanently. Alone.

I'd watched him for three days while I was there. He was sipping his soup in solitude, nervously ripping his chapati apart and slowly stuffing it into his mouth.

He always dined by himself. Mistreating waiters; brooding in silence. More depressed than Death Valley.

I couldn't make out his nationality until the last day when I finally sensed he might be Italian. So I spoke to him and he lit up, his back straightened. A fellow countryman, someone to talk to! That's what he must've thought. And he poured it all out.

His name was Giacinto, he was a top engineer working on a drilling platform in the Bay of Bengal for an Italian multinational. He'd fly in a helicopter almost every day, out there in the middle of the oceanic nowhere.

He couldn't get along with his Indian counterparts, couldn't get things done. By being miserable, he made it impossible for his project to speed up, not knowing how to decode the Indian culture. He was lengthening his own miserable stay, because of the fact of being miserable.

*

In 1905, Charles Woodruff, an American white-supremacist doctor working in the Philippines wrote a book called *The Effects of Tropical Light on White Man*. It mostly documented his fears about the threats to the blond Aryan race, which he obviously considered superior to all others, as he theorized that white men in the tropics suffer from what is known at 'Tropical Neurasthenia'.

In a 300-page, quasi-scientific treatise, he explained how corpuscles and electrons, Hertzian, infra-red and ultra-violet waves, along with radium rays, could impact the function of sensory nerves, along with sunstrokes and retinal irritation in lighter-skinned migrants who moved to tropical areas.

Although admitting that Romantic poet Shelley depended upon the stimulus of light and wrote his best poetry on the roof of his house near Livorno, 'entirely unscreened from the pelting rays of the hottest Italian sun', and that Byron was 'no less a sun-worshipper, who noticed remarkable changes in feeling on sunny days', and listing the fact that even 'Rousseau, like Shelley, loved to expose his bare head to the sun's fiercest rays even in the hottest weather', and Goethe speaks of his 'sun thirst' which Walt Whitman also experienced by writing 'while lying in the hot sunshine on the white sands of the seashore', the danger of heat fever can actually lead vellais, who stay too long in tropical climates and light, to 'incompetence, melancholia, paranoia, nervousness, alcoholism, and sexual deviance'.

There's even a theory about the East India Company by colonial historian Kim Wagner stating that: 'British brutality could be explained and even justified with reference to the climate, physical exhaustion and, ultimately, the savagery ascribed to their Indian victims.' So you see, it was the sun and the locals' 'savagery' which provoked them into being so fierce, really.

The heat striking the enlarged 'superior brains' of these vellais, 'harnessed anxiety about masculinity and the purity and superiority of the white race and put failure in the supposedly moral project of the Empire down to the local climate and population, rather than colonials themselves,' as *The Guardian* columnist Afua Hirsch has analyzed.

But the conclusion of *The Effects of Tropical Light on White Men*, in chapter XIII titled 'Practical Rules for White Men in the Tropics' (most useful: wear white clothes by day, dark ones at night) is simply that 'acclimatization is impossible,' 'neurasthenic states are due to excessive metabolism caused by light' as the British Army knew well, since it limited the tour of duty into southern India for white soldiers to no more than five years, and never sent officers over 50 to these regions for fear of 'Tropical Neurasthenia'.

*

So fellow whiteys, you are now warned, about the side effects of your wandering life in the Tropics…However, there are also deep advantages, to the nomadic life, if you know how to nurture them.

When you move to a new culture you are more likely to be forced to define who you are. You have to ask yourself if what you identify with is really you or just the result of the influence of the culture you grew up in.

In a new environment, you are forced to question your values and beliefs, to either strengthen them or get rid of them. It's not how many countries you live in, it's how long you live abroad.

What good does it do to define who you are? Well, if you are convinced already you are a superior blond Aryan and suffer from Tropical Neurasthenia, there's little hope for you. But in case you are not in this category, and you question who you are and wish to attain a clearer sense of self, you could be more likely to shorten the distance between the perception you have of yourself and that which others have of you.

It is thus more likely you will formulate better decisions, since you'll know what options better match your characteristics.

What's not really clear is if people who live in foreign cultures are more likely to have a clearer sense of self or people with a clearer sense of self are more likely to live abroad.

Of course, all this works if you get over that anxiety that comes from losing all your familiar context, if you overpower the initial culture shock. Otherwise you get stuck in constant anxiety.

*

For example, you can run into Italians who are shocked that you eat Indian food with your fingers, who think sitting on the floor is weird, who don't understand sleeping on the floor doesn't mean you're miserable nor dirt poor.

The most banal, obvious first comment is: 'Oh, I arrived in Kolkata and saw so many people sleeping on the street. Oh, my God, it's so saaaad…'

And although homelessness is a huge problem in India, sleeping on the floor, here, does not carry the same social stigma as it has in Stuttgart, Valencia, or Modena.

You can also run into that Italian couple who hates

living in Chennai, only hangs out with other Italians, can't make friends with the locals, nor do they want to, is always aggressive and suspicious with the vendor at the vegetable shop in the corner—always feels like 'they' are trying to cheat 'us'.

You may run into them at a Brunello di Montalcino tasting in some posh hotel, with some Tuscanian count in a bespoke suit, and they invite you to their house to roast a little suckling pig they were able to procure for themselves from this butcher they found.

When you finally introduce to them your hybrid wife, they blurt out their racism by saying: 'Oh, but you're so beautifulah, you don't really lookah Indian. And you are not Tamil, right? No, you don't look Tamil, you're so beautifullah.'

As if being Tamil, one of the most symmetrical and smooth skinned people you will find in this planet, didn't fall under the universal canon of beauty. I think I should send them a copy of Charles Woodruff's book.

I look at the Italian lady's bleached blond hair and wrinkles, at her husband's wispy hair coming out of the big nostrils and the receding hairline and pronounce my '*addio*' which in Italian means 'goodbye forever'. Suckers.

How do you see me?

The stupid vellai with the Anglo-mestizo

How do my Indian friends see us expats, us lost souls in a distant land?

There's that reaction I have when I see whiteys after many months in Tamil Nadu. My friends here must have the same feeling.

I get a sense of that, mixed with a good dose of straight-out ageism, at the annual Christmas party Divya invites my wife and I to at her father's house.

I'm almost 10 years older than my wife, but innocently never perceived that to be a problem. Then again, I also don't perceive us as being what is called a mixed marriage.

But this is my blindness. To some people, we appear as a differently aged, mixed marriage couple. Whitey with mixed local. Caucasian with Anglo-mestizo. Late 40s dude with late 30s chick, type of reasoning.

In India, my being white makes me look older by juxtaposition to the locals which is something I realize only at the party.

As we've been going on spin-doctoring our own lives, appearing as that 'writers couple', living in that picture perfect commercial for our own lives that is Arlanymor, I thought everything was fine and normal.

But that postcard-perfect shot I have in my mind is

not that perfect, as seen through the eyes of someone like Divya, who is younger than my wife, and, at this party, a bit drunker than both my wife and I.

She insists, stunned, in reminding me of this real fact:

'You know, Carlo,' she slurs, 'you know, if you think about it, you are closer in age to my father than you are to me, right? Isn't that weird? Isn't that weird? It is weird, right? Right? Right?'

Buzz off, Divya…But she is right, of course. And it stands out even more because I'm that vellai mappillai.

How could I not see it?

It takes me months to digest that. Not only am I ageing, the pepper getting drowned by the salt in my hair, the belly plopping back out as soon as I stop walking 10 km or running 5 km a day, but it's all happening in a country where many of my peers look way younger than me.

'I went to this great party in Goa,' screamed Constantino, known as Tino, when he reached our table in South Goa, once. 'All young people! There was no one older than 40! It was just great…'

I took it as a compliment that he didn't think the white hair in my beard put me above 50, in what is popularly perceived as 'uncle territory'. But I felt the sting.

Ageism in India, yes. No country for old men. 'Didn't use to be.' But isn't this phrase exactly the kind of thing that old men say?

It just may be that this India is rebelling against the concept of forced respect for the elderly which is imposed by a tradition that is felt as repressing and constraining. An anti-Aunties, anti-Uncles rebellion is brewing?

Look for the signs. They are there.

*

'Oh yes,' says Harri one afternoon, when we're hanging out on a beach south of Chennai, chatting away. 'To us you look like one of the yoga-people. Most whiteys who come to India for a vacation are yoga-people. They are not necessarily all old. But they are all sick, man. Think about it. What are they doing here? Trying to heal, finding healing, wellness. So it means they are all sick, right? But they can't heal because they are neurotic cases. Trust me, I used to date one. They seem all "shanti, shanti, om" but you rub the surface and find a mess. They don't know where they're at, dude. They're sad, forcing themselves to be happy. Lots of work. Sweating in those tight Lycra pants? Woah. Mostly they end up injuring their backs and knees, in the long run. Yoga-people. Keep away. Trouble.'

So, I prod him:

'This is how you see me? This is how you all see me? Because I came here as yoga-people myself, you know? Mysore, Patthabi Jois, meditating, learning the mantras, singing bhajans in a temple in Tiruvannamalai, and all that...'

Harri gives me a pearl of honesty that I find unacceptable to hear:

'No, man. You want to know the truth, the whole truth, really, about what these people, these Tamil people think about you?' he says pointing to the Saturday afternoon crowd of smiling Tamilians, strolling alone, in couples or in families up and down this idyllic urban beach on the south of Chennai.

'You wanna know?'

'Yes, I do.'

'They think you are better than them.'

'What?'

'Yeah, man. That's the truth. They might not admit it. But that's what they think.'

'But why?'

'Because you are freer. You are mentally freer. You are more modern, you are more courageous, you have less hang ups than we have.'

'You think so?'

'I know so. We have so many obligations. To family, friends, colleagues, to society. We have so much pressure. We must succeed, we must marry, we must do this, we must do that. You don't. You represent that freedom we want, but we still don't have. You are better. And we envy you for that. Inevitable.'

I feel very embarrassed by this concept. I can't accept it. My egalitarian soul won't take it.

Although it explains Divya's issues towards our age difference, and certain strange attitudes exhibited by some of my wife's Chennai peers, which I had attributed to their suppressed rage for my having dragged one of Chennai's most lovely and eligible to the altar.

'You are exaggerating...' I try to say, very uneasy in this role of envied self-reliant, wind-in-my-hair, do-what-I-damn-please whitey prototype he's trying to cast me in.

But Harri has a point. And he drives it to its uncomfortable end.

'And you know what? I mean, do you want to know something about those people who think that?'

'Yes? What?'

'They are right. You are superior. Because you are freer.'

Oh, man, I can't take this. Is he really saying this?

'Yes, most of the time the vellai is better than them, in this sense. No one wants to admit it in their pride, but that's what it is, bro.'

I love Harri for his courage to admit something so lucidly delineated and so difficult to face. But I hate the conclusion he arrives at. And it leaves me pondering on this racial dilemma for many years to come.

*

Why are there so many vellais here in India now? It depends.

Are they secretly here to enjoy that white-men privilege and covert envy/admiration Harri just spelled out for me?

Has there been a resurgence of migration here from so-called civilized countries, as New India began its gallop into economic growth, first slow then fast then again, post-demonetization and the painful GST tax reform, slow again? For sure.

I think of the veterans of this identity: white people who moved to India after 1947. Like the dreamers of Auroville, the psychedelic trancers of Goa, the left-over hippies of Rishikesh, or the Ashtanga yogis of Mysore and Pune, the meditators in the many ashrams, followers of many gurus, from Osho to Sai Baba to the hugging Amma, or the students of the Vedas, Sanskrit, Indian music and dance, but also the focused businessmen in the metal industries, building harbours, dredging canals or in IT, the ones who come to build a solar panel empire or the gallery owners in Delhi, the fashionistas who've come to savour the promise of a future in India, just like the voluntourists who have come to taste the charisma of an icon of the past in one of Mother Teresa's houses in Kolkata, the City of Joy, and the charity thrills that come with it.

There are also those who pitch their tents in the

tourism industry, running a funky, elegant hotel in South Goa or Chettinad, or a chain of trendy hotels all over India. Or sports legends, the washed-up gladiators of the European or Brazilian soccer championships who come to embolden the hopes of the Indian Super League like super-stars Zico, Alessandro Del Piero or Marco Materazzi.

Among them you'll find those whiteys who can't integrate and slide back into a resentful isolation, those who hang out only among expats and see India through the thick transparent glass of expensive hotels or gated communities, or you may find those who go native and never take off their kurtas, even in Europe or in America, those who are here to be what they really are, to fulfil a frustrated potential.

Take my friend William, for example, my Zodiac brother. He's become a literary legend, writes dreamy and well-researched books, often dipped in unknown aspects of this great sub-continent. He also co-founded and manages one of the most successful literary festivals in the world. He's a vulcan of energy, ideas, ebullience and enthusiasm.

'He's finally learned how to be among Indians,' says a Dilliwalla friend.

Once, at the beginning of my Indian life, when my wife and I were still considering spending half of the year in the expensive, yet reassuringly hygenized and organized West, he advised me otherwise:

'Stay here, Carlo. Actually, move to Delhi, where the action is. Do you think I would've been able to write the books I've published, to start a literary festival, move to a farm, live the life I live if I'd stayed in the UK? Maybe, but I doubt it. India is a good place for people like us. It's a place full of wonderful opportunities. A good place to be in this moment in history too.'

I now fully agree with him. Not just from a historical and geopolitical point of view, realizing that at this juncture of world events, this incredible sleeping giant is in a moment of transformation that is exciting to witness. And that its role in Asia and the rest of the world, is really growing. But also from a personal, intimate point of view.

It is much more stimulating to be in a country filled with hopes and optimism about the future, even though its present is plagued by growing intolerance and inequality, than being in the agony and slow decadence of a Europe that can clearly acknowledge the next decade cannot be better than the previous 50 years. Or an America that is turning its eagle beak towards an imaginary jingoistic, isolationist past.

That's also why some of us whiteys are here. This is why William is here. Although he somewhat dodged the pitfalls of going native, maybe because of that old Commonwealth syndrome which never allows for truly full integration.

The best example of the going native for me is my colleague, the late Tiziano Terzani, an Italian best-selling author and correspondent from India.

He'd visited and lived in other Asian countries, but found his home here. Hated Japan, loved India where he was diagnosed with an incurable cancer and slowly prepared to die.

He would arrive back in Italy sporting a long sadhu-like white beard and hair, long white kurta and pantaloons. His look communicated to the Italians of the '90s the solitary cave of meditation they thought he was emerging from, bringing with him pearls of wisdom some people took in as being worthy of a Ramana Maharishi.

He was welcomed by growing crowds as a guru, wrote about his spiritual relationship with the afterlife and found success and adoration from the readers of his best-sellers.

I always found that he was putting up the mask of the Indianized Italian because it worked. Not because of any shrewd, opportunistic calculation, but simply because, first of all, he liked it, and, secondly, because he thought his message would get across better.

And because he had found rest for his ebullient, Tuscan dislike for a contemporary Italy, much as I have, in the splendid non-attachment of Vedic thought, and in the sattvic company of the Indian vibe.

Sometimes you have to work on your mask to

make the delivery of your message more efficient. That's all.

The trendy, dread-locked Italian Rastafarian types, with a Shiva trident tattooed on their chest, the 30-something Italians who manufacture the best chillums in the market seem like less charismatic carbon copies of that Terzani, who was and still is, through the books he left behind, bringing to his readers and followers some hope for the afterlife, some peaceful acceptance of death.

I don't judge those who wear their salwar kameez in Italy, France, London, New York or Boulder. Or who show up looking like a Caucasian Punjabi in the Milan metro, just like I have no problem with the saffron-clad Hare Krishna either.

They miss India, that's all. But I would venture to diagnose that, in most cases, it's a simple case of culture shock's side effects.

I find more honest those like William, who found in India a treasure chest filled with stories and transformed them in successful books. Vellais who contributed, with their love of knowledge, to provide an extra point of view on a millennial history that constantly has something to teach to the world.

These are the kind of vellais who have come to stay. Forever, for a while, doesn't matter.

They are serious, committed.

They will understand their India reality and experience deeply.

Not like the voluntourists you can meet in Kolkata, if you spend a day cleaning up vomit and piss from guests in one of Mother Teresa's houses, like I did.

Voluntouring with Mother Teresa's nuns in Kolkata...

...while I get a phone call from my wife modelling for a magazine

'You are giving me too little notice! Tomorrow? You must send a written request and we'll consider it. It's clear you really don't understand much of what we are doing here. But, anyway, give me a written request. I'll see what I can do. Show up here at mass at 6 am tomorrow and we'll see if you can work as a volunteer for us.'

I was beginning to see why Sister Blessiella, in charge of receiving visitors at Mother House in Kolkata, had earned the nickname of Mother Cerberus. A real pain in the ass.

'Suffering is a gift from God,' Mother Teresa used to say, so I humbly comply and follow protocol, apologizing profusely and piously.

The morning after, at dawn, the streets are deserted and so is the alley where you can find Mother House. In the first courtyard, a gray statue of the Saint extends a hand, palm down, while pilgrims kneel to receive blessings from an inanimate object.

I've come to experience a day as a volunteer. I've been asked to write about Mother Teresa on the anniversary of her birthday. What I discover is that the white volunteers are here mostly on a personal quest, although some are moved by a sincere religious calling.

It's all a flurry of nuns in white saris and pilgrims praying and singing in a mass celebrated by a young priest.

Next to the sepulchre, in a room with a bench and a poster collecting Mother's sayings and lessons, believers walk clock-wise, stopping to kneel and pray, presenting miracle requests, leaning their forehead on the marble of the tomb, humming more prayers.

In the middle of the marble slab there's a mound of rose petals shaped like a heart. Some followers approach the tomb, swipe up a handful of those petals, and eat them, like a consecrated host. Mother Teresa's real name, in fact, in Albanian means 'little Rose'.

And here come the volunteers, mostly Spaniards from Madrid, a group of 45 people on the last 24 hours of their 18 days of volunteering service. *Toulgrims*: tourist-pilgrims.

Women with braids in their hair, wearing t-shirts and printed cotton pants that scream 'coming from yoga class.' Men with ungainly capri pants and, unfortunately, yes, ponytails.

It's hot. Too hot. It's Kolkata. It's the end of August.

I'm on the verge of changing my mind about this Mother Teresa volunteering business which, as every Bengali knows, highly misrepresents a contextually well-off Kolkata, a regal metropolis which suffers from dated international stereotypes of urban misery.

Too late. We're off for a 40 minutes march through the slums, dodging auto rickshaws, police jeeps, trains, cow dung, cows, men soaping up in collective showers, children making fun of the marching foreigners, roofless stables, mountains of trash everywhere, crowds hopping off passenger trains.

It all seems so well choreographed.

I must be patient. The City of Joy will give some joys.

Finally, metal gates open up to us 'Prem Dan House—dying and afflicted', as Mother Cerberus had recited, as if reading the options for the day off a menu.

As I inch into the courtyard, I observe mutilated older folks with gauze bandages still stained with iodine and other disabled men sitting out in the open under a wide corrugated roof, catching the breeze. The most serious cases are kept inside a large dormitory where we'll have to clean up all the vomit, faeces, and urine.

A man, skeleton legs and arms, sleeps under the blanket, nursing a stomach with a deformation as big as a newborn baby. Another, crumpled on the floor, is refusing to get up.

There's no time to linger in awe of the suffering. The volunteers must now climb up to the roof.

I'm ordered to wear an apron and for two hours, sporting a Steve Van Zandt meets Guns'n'Roses blue handkerchief to shield my head from the sun, I start squeezing shorts, t-shirts, shirts, lungis, sheets and towels, laying them out to dry on a line, under the burning Bengal sun.

Three Spanish boys are deeply immersed in a philosophical chat.

'For me, man is fundamentally good,' says Francisco, a starry-eyed, short Catalan wearing a bracelet which reads 'say no to the new drug'. 'It's pornography,' he explains. Another bracelet says 'Francisco loves Jesus', a souvenir of a Catholic youth camp in Poland.

Lucas, dopey, emaciated, but with a cheeky glance, is skeptical: 'I don't believe in a superior being. I believe there are enlightened humans like Mother Teresa, people who have changed some things in the world. But I don't believe in the Christian god. However,' he concludes, giving a strong pat on his friend's back, 'if there is a hell, it must have a VIP lounge for Catalans!'

At this point everyone perceives the beginning of a growing energy and euphoria: the more difficult and humiliating the tasks, the stronger the inner voltage.

Alfonso, an overweight, overeager and over-chatty Basque man, roams among the afflicted, offering to clip fingernails on both hands and feet.

Andreas, a white-haired, curved Argentinian who seems to have survived a few Psy-Goa trance raves, seems happy to empty pitchers full of urine, after he and I have made up the beds for half the dormitory, pulling sheets and stuffing pillows in their cases among sick patients in dialysis, some without an eye, with malformations on their arms or legs, but all of them with wide smiles, compulsively greeting the foreigners with vigorous handshakes. 'Hello, how are you doing?'

Although we've been prohibited from bringing cell phones, I suddenly feel a vibration in my pocket.

'Hello?'

'It's not going well here!' my wife complains.

She's in a 5-star hotel nearby, here in Kolkata, posing as a model for a video and a photoshoot commissioned by some big Condé Nast magazine.

I feel odd imagining her in our luxurious suite, high up on the top floors, overlooking in the distance the very same slum where I am. I look up to that glass tower as I speak to her.

'I'm sorry to hear that, love,' I say.

'I'm so frustrated! They are making me do things I don't feel really represent me, you know?'

'Yes…I can understand, but…I'm sorry, it's a bit odd for me to relate deeply to this problem considering where I am, you see…'

'Oh, yeah, I know. Right…But what should I do? They are making my hair look horrible, all poofy and bouffant!'

'Poofy? Well, tell them you won't do that. Just stand your ground. No bouffant!'

'I should, right?'

'You should. But I have to go now because I'm actually not allowed to be on the phone,' I say, as an older nun gives me the 'You heathen, I will burn in mobile phone hell' look.

I quickly hang up as the nun orders me to carry inside a piss-reeking bed laid out in the sun. A volunteer named Pilar tells me that in a few days she'll have to get back to work as a secretary in a notary's office in Madrid.

'This in an experience that changes you,' she says at chai break. 'The first three days it was total shock. I didn't think I'd make it. Indiaaaah…the heat, the noise, the strong smell, the dogs, the crows, the food. Trauma. After three days I got used to it. I go home, happy to return, you know? Not like after my sea-side vacations in Malaga, where the end of my summer break is always depressing, because you'd rather stay at the beach that go back to work…'

'No, it's not like leaving Malaga, no,' I agree with her. Voluntourism? Yes, a bit.

I get the feeling some of these people hang out here for two or three weeks, *chez* Mother Teresa, not because of a vocation, a need to heal people, but because of the experience so they can say they've done it.

So they can feel better once they are home. How sick is that?

Andy is a typically fair and perpetually sunburnt German who rolls out his travel plan. Mother House seems like just one more exotic stop: 'Next, Varanasi. Then Mumbai, by train. I've come to have an experience. I'm not very religious. But I've come here to understand. Seeing people who sleep in the open, being here every day—it's shocking, really. Indiaaah…But you're getting emotional about it, about your own empathy, isn't going to help anyone, is it? Here you can do something pragmatic. And I think it will be useful for me once I'm back in Germany, when things don't work out how I'd like them to, or when I'm about to get mad because I can't find a WiFi connection or a Starbucks at the corner… well, then I'll remember that I helped an old man by shaving his trembling jaw, once, in Kolkata, you know?'

Yes, the dying and afflicted as a cure against the frustration caused by the lack of a Starbucks—I understand, Andy, *alles klar*.

Lucas at one point blurts out his truth: 'After three weeks here, it's always the same ol' thing. It's boring!'

Andreas gets angry at three volunteers taking pictures with their phones: 'Does it look like a place for selfies? Really?!' he screams with sanctimonious frustration and his Argentinean cockiness.

The day has been long, but yet, at the end, although I'm not a believer, I realize I'm not tired, I actually feel more strength and energy than I did in the morning at 6 am. This is the secret drug that volunteers come here for, whether they realize it or not. This quasi-spiritual jolt.

And, yet, I'm so happy to hop into an Uber and get the driver to take me back to that 5-star's bathtub with a bird's-eye view of Kolkata to listen to conceptual problems created by a fashion shoot.

Forgive me, Mother Teresa.

*

Many people in the West, which I think technically starts in Greece and, flying towards the sunset, ends in Australia, are a bit puzzled by Not-So-New India when they are considering giving money to help its poor.

Why should I send my money to help them? Why shave off my dwindling salary to help Indian women with local inequalities?

I mean, India is not so poor any longer. Everyone knows that, by now.

Plus, it seems like Delhi uses its funds to send satellites of other countries up in space, for a hefty fee, or to finance a nuclear program. What about the eight submarines bought from the Russians? What about the billionaire contracts to either build, import or provide arms, cannons, ships, aircraft and more and more weapons, so much so that India these days has reached the highest defence investment budget in the world?

It's hard to balance this heavy fact with the need to help 600 million people get a toilet. To feed the hungry when floods or droughts hit and kill, as they keep on doing.

Why should Westerners feel morally responsible for this situation of inequality that creates suffering? Colonization, which, at any rate, was a specific British responsibility, technically ended in 1947.

As is the case everywhere else in the world, hunger is a matter of politics, not lack of resources. It is a matter of inequality, of millions of people living in conditions of virtual slavery, often indebted to their employers and chained by such onus to their 'owners' forever. Modern slavery. All this in India, which the Constitution still defines as a Socialist Republic.

Good souls need to feel their own lives have meaning by exercising the humane act of helping those in need. Even if it's a secretary who barely gets by in Madrid. Or a student still unemployed from the South of Germany.

What better expression of that human need than the emaciated beggars of Kolkata?

Mother Teresa must've known that. And it doesn't mean Christopher Hitchens was right in trying to take down her myth in his exposé *Missionary Position*.

It means that she must've known that the neurotic need to feel better about yourself, to come and experience the deep discomforts of a challenging life, would help Westerners appreciate what they have back home much more easily.

Is it wrong?

Is it deceitful and opportunistic to manipulate such feelings?

My countryman Niccolò Machiavelli would answer no, because the Sisters of Mother Teresa are NOT secretly buying villas in the South of France, where they go riding around with young gigolos in the summer.

They are NOT, as far as we know, embezzling funds to speculate in cryptocurrency or some other selfish goal. They are actually using the money to help the poor and needy in Kolkata, in India, and in the world, wherever they operate.

No one has proved the contrary, as far as I know.

Does it matter that they put on a bit of a show by letting hundreds of people come to their houses of suffering and ailing people to do work that would be much more easily done by the locals? Not really.

Let's just call it what it is: customer retention.

You come, you see our lepers, our dying customers, you can be close to them, you do your horror-tour and are then forced to think about that.

You give your time, your money, and get to feel a bond with this restricted view of Indiaaaah.

With this limited impact you can have, it all works out fine because, in the end, no one was harmed, no one was duped (except the voluntourists duping themselves into not seeing this mechanism) and some good was done.

Which is all that counts.

Latin lovers in India

'Italians good people, good workers, good musicians, good singers, famed Latin lovers, yes...sorry...but not good fighters '

I have to confess something to you.

I'm not the first person in my family who's moved to India for a few years.

I am also not the first writer in my family to have written about his experiences in India in a book.

Earlier, I mentioned the veteran vellais: white people in India after 1947. But white people, as you all know, have been living here, mostly uninvited, even before 1947.

My relative was one of them. Only he was not—as you may think—one of the oppressors. He was not here as a colonial officer, or a worker helping to fill the coffers of the East India Company, a lackey of the British Empire.

He was here as their prisoner. A prisoner of war.

Here is the story of my great-uncle Otto, brother of my Nonna Mari, a talented oil painter and pianist who reached the age of 98 and taught me a lot about life.

Even before becoming a vellai mappillai, I was convinced that ancestors are important, should be respected—when they deserve to, not unconditionally—and should be remembered.

They serve a purpose that goes beyond the spiritual. They can help us find within ourselves some of the qualities they have been able to foster and express.

If they left a good memory, they left a good example. And this is useful to those who are still alive.

Memory can help us go through life as stronger and smarter individuals or collective groups, like families. And even if some people who have lived before us are not related to us, their example can still comfort us. Especially if they have lived and thrived in more challenging historical eras.

If *they* could do it during war, famine, colonialism, slavery, why can't *I* today? Their example can make our latent qualities blossom.

Uncle Ottone was not a purely positive example. He was prone to loud temper tantrums against his wife and children.

He made up for it by also being a loving, kind, enthusiastic and generous man. And by being a prized poet blessed with the quality of courage, a characteristic that proved indispensable as a prisoner of war of the British Army for six years in India.

There is a trace of Ottone's audacity in the Indian press as well.

I found this fragment carefully glued to his Indian journals, a precious collection of thoughts, some analysis of Indian culture and ideas that I've had access to.

It's a clipping from a Bangalore English language newspaper dated 10 August 1941 and it says:

Escaped Italians Arrested

Anantapur, Aug. 9

Four Italian prisoners were captured yesterday by the Dharmavaram police at Chignicherla and brought here. One of the prisoners, who spoke English, stated that they were officers who had escaped from the Bangalore camp to study the country and that they were on their way to Mormugao. The Superintendent of Police is awaiting further instructions.— F.O.C.

I remember very vividly the image of my great-uncle Ottone Menato riding his bicycle through the main road of the sleepy small city where I grew up.

He must've been in his late 60s by then, but was still lean, muscular, always sporting a leathery mountain tan and ready to flash a charismatic smile that lured you towards him and to his aura of a man with a real past.

He was a known alpinist who had given colourful names to valleys and vertical rock climbing routes. Mostly, he was a novelist, which had always been my vocation as well. We exchanged short stories at one point, before he died.

His most famous novel contains the secret of my fascination with him: it's the tale of six years in three

British prison camps during World War II—first briefly in Egypt, where he'd been captured, but mostly in India's Bangalore and the Dharamsala-Yol camps.

I still smile when I think of the humour he demonstrated by calling his novel *Latin Lovers*. There's hardly a woman in the book, except for the main character's wife, to whom in long letters he confesses his longings, sufferings and frustrations, also documenting his spiritual quest and probing existential questions; and then a local Indian woman who sold her body to prisoners.

The title refers to a conversation on the very last page of the novel—Captain Diego Taranto of the Alpini Mountain Corps is intent on smashing some rocks, mostly to vent his rage at still being in captivity after the war has ended and after six years have passed since his capture, when he's approached by a Dravidian clerk on his day off to celebrate 'V-day'.

The clerk tells him with a smile that the war is over and that the POWs can finally go home. Diego is in no mood and ignores him rudely. But the clerk insists and goes for the jugular:

'Italians...sorry...yes, Italians good! Good people, good workers, good musicians, good singers, famed Latin lovers, yes...sorry...but not good fighters.'

So Diego just tells him rudely to leave him the heck alone. It is exactly for that reason that Diego (like his creator, Ottone) had kept trying to escape, risking his life, for years—to prove that he was somewhat better than that demeaning international stereotype.

I find it such a poignant ending for a book which recounts how in the battle of Tobruk, in Northern Africa, the Italians were badly equipped and quickly beaten and captured.

Diego escapes from the Egyptian prison, survives for weeks, gets caught and shipped across the Indian Ocean to Bombay. Then, on bolted train cars, he's transferred to a Bangalore officers' POWs camp.

As the fictional Capt. Diego Taranto begins to successfully prepare his many escapes (getting regularly captured), we read of an India in the years of Partition and Independence, where most of the locals encountered do not consider the Italian prisoners on the run as hostile, but treat them as any other exotic and peaceful foreign guest would be treated.

Once Diego has escaped a couple of times and survives solitary confinement (just like my uncle Ottone had), the news of Japanese troops moving towards Singapore forces the British to move the prison at the feet of the Himalayas, near Dharamshala, in a camp called Yol, meaning, 'Young Officers on Leave', an impressive citadel with hundreds of barracks on a 770 acres property.

Diego manages to run away again, summoned by

the magnetism of the beloved mountains. Uncle Ottone wrote that it was an officer's duty to escape, no matter how hopeless the endeavour: 'It was the only way a prisoner could keep the enemy busy.' How contrary to the Italian stereotype.

I can't hide the pride I feel in his attempt to be something else, not the common trope of the Ulysses-like, cunning Mediterranean who uses his wits more than his heart, but a man with clean, honest valour who made it through some tough winters, up there in the Himalayan barracks.

Yol still stands. From August to October 1947, 12,000 Indian Muslims were kept there on their way to Pakistan. From 1949 to 1952 it became a refugee camp for Kashmiri migrants. Then, it was turned into military barracks, housing the youngest battalion of the Indian Army—Rising Star. People still report finding old rusted cans used by the Italians. They are a memento of a painful chapter in history.

A painful season of life that my great-uncle tried to exorcise from his nervous system by writing a novel, to cope with a trauma and transform a memory into something useful for himself and for others.

A worthwhile lesson for a writer.

How to become a Reverse Coconut

How an AADHAAR card can get you a discount in a Kovalam restaurant ten years later. A most unusual eye-sight check-up, among doctors and fixers in a jungle of forms and queues. And how caste grumpiness led me to accept my dharma.

My past self of 2008 meets myself in 2018

'No, no photo! Tourist ille! I have an AADHAAR card, dammit!'

Back to the same beach 10 years later…

This morning the hawkers in Adimalathura beach, near Kovalam in Kerala, are just beyond unbearable.

'Hello, hello? *Wunderbar!*' The guy points to a handful of carved marble spheres he thinks you cannot live without.

'No, no, leave me alone.'

'Maybe later?'

He moves over to another umbrella. Soon, I hear the scream of a distressed Italian lady, who probably has had just one pint too many of Ayurvedic oil smeared on her mozzarella coloured skin, and is about to lose it.

'Noh, noh, noh, noh, no, "maybe later!" Nothing "later". I never make a promise that I can't keep! I don't want to buy anything now, and I don't want to buy anything later. Ok? *Basta!*'

Yes, culture clash.

But, unfortunately, I agree with her.

This Kerala beach is a prime target for hawkers pushing bric-a-brac on guilt-ridden pallid tourists.

I think of all the bribing and exchanges of favours in order to obtain the authorization to come here to bother tourists who, after breakfast, descend the long staircase from the Somatheeram Ayurveda Village, or the more picturesque Travancore Heritage hotel.

This is a prime spot to sell useless souvenirs and fruits to hapless tourists braving skin cancer and drying their European dampness from their limbs and glands.

After 10 years, in February 2018, I've finally returned to Kovalam, on the southernmost tip of India. This is where I spent New Year's Eve 10 years ago, the day after meeting my wife to be.

I was hanging out at this very same beach, and, as I look at the umbrellas and chaises longues, I remember the fireworks on 31 December 2008.

Who was I then?

Who was I, when I first came here?

How come I have changed so much?

And, have I?

How dreamy everything was.

Every ripple in the waves, every hue in the clouds, every distant sound, like that of the boys chanting and dancing together at the beach in their oneiric silhouettes cast against the shining sea surface—an image that, 10 years later, I still carry with me, and somewhere in a hard-drive, in the shape of a portable phone video file.

I was a tourist then. But now?

'Tourist ille!!!' I yell impatiently at the poor, yet mildly annoying middle-aged lady who, within 10 minutes, has already come three times to my circular shadow oasis, trying to sell me fruits. Luckily Tamil and Malayalam languages are close enough.

She's brandishing a long knife, which I'm sure she feels like slicing me with, instead of the out of season mangoes she's peddling.

'Mangoes? Mangoes?! Really?! You are trying to sell me mangos? It's not mango season, lady! Don't you think I know? Mango season starts in March, in April, and ends in August. It's February! Who do you think I am?'

'Papaya, maybe?'

'I already had lots of papaya for breakfast, thank you. Bye.'

'Banana, maybe?'

'Tourist ille! I've had my morning vitamins already! I'm local. I live here. I earn my salary in rupees and you want to sell me some overpriced fruits I don't want? I have an AADHAAR card, dammit! Just leave me alone. Local vellai, ok?'

I know it's hard for my mom to understand, as she looks at me with dismay, lounging right next to me on this beach. (I'm Italian, I travel with my mother even as an adult, yes.) It's hard for her to understand my reaction, when a pudgy man wearing a candid, well ironed and starched white shirt starts stomping down the beach dune, heading towards us, brandishing his phone like it's a national flag on Republic Day.

I know where this is going.

He gestures towards his phone, flashing his big smile: 'Photo, photo, photo with me!'

I whip out the biggest Tamil mappillai smile I can muster, and repeat my litany: 'Tourist ille, buddy. I live here. I'm a local.

I ain't about to stop to get my picture taken with every dude who wants to use me as their little white clown. I've had it.

'No thanks, I live here. I won't stop my walk to have my picture taken with every Indian tourist I run into, I'm past that, sorry, gotta go, you're breaking my stride, brah.'

My mother is horrified by my grumpy rudeness.

I remember what that American lady said to me, once, about the white man screaming at the top of his lungs in a post office queue, at some point of life in India, and that man will be you.

But it's different, as I try to explain.

'I live here, *mamma*, I've been living here for almost 10 years now, right? There's only an hour before sunset to take our walk on the beach. If we stop out of courtesy for every naive Indian tourist who thinks that just because you're white you belong in their photograph, we'll never make it, sorry, *mi dispiace, mamma*.'

She's not fully convinced, wrapped in her shining red bathing suit, cloaked in her red Indian shawl, shaded by her wide-rimmed red beach hat—a redly attired grandma from Italy.

As a reverse coconut, I can definitely understand why people want to be photographed with her. Or to pose next to that vellai with a straw hat and funky big 'coolers', skilfully brandishing a cane to keep stray dogs away (I've gone native on that one too).

But no thanks, *nandri*.

Thanks, but no thanks, tourist *ille*.

This is how I've changed.

My lackadaisical desire to fit in, my harmonious yogic self of the year 2008 has given way to a much more Indian middle class attitude.

If I picture myself back then, on this very same Kerala beach, I see a younger Carlo who moves more gracefully, slowly, who wakes up every morning at dawn to meditate for 30 minutes and then does his Ashtanga yoga asanas for another hour and emerges in a relaxed bliss.

A taciturn, melancholic dreamer escaping the Western mode, looking for peace in India, on a spiritual quest to figure out what spiritual even means.

Yes, a caricature of those Orientalists who come to find out 'who they aaare' perhaps.

I confess: I was one of those folks who saw India as a simplified spiritual playground, in naive awe of the patience, the smiles, the harmony, in admiration of the calmness, trying to learn from it, maybe slightly going native too. One of those who thought all Indians are innately more spiritual...Right.

In those first three months in India, in 2008, I was living a marvellous dream. Everything was a lesson, a transcendental message to be interpreted and be taken as an indication on how to lead a different life, how to change. I was blindly in love with India.

Then came the settling in. The moving to Chennai. The becoming a local who can now shout away the hawkers by brandishing his AADHAAR card and who, by the way, just saying, got 300 rupees knocked off a black pomfret fish at the Coconut Grove tourist trap restaurant in Kovalam! Thanks to his AADHAAR digital biometric identity card. Don't say they're useless!

Settling in came at a cost.

First and foremost, the customary Tipu Sultan's revenge, which to me is the South Indian version of the notorious Montezuma's revenge, which I had already experienced in Mexico.

Yes, disgusting, I know: bowel issues.

It took my mind a bit of time to get settled in my first couple of years in India. It took my body a bit longer.

Lucky for me, I had moved to one of India's medical capitals.

My days of hospital tourism

Or how I was diagnosed with having Indian eyes

The doctor peering into my eye-bulbs with a magnifying lens through a microscope seems puzzled by what he sees.

'Do you have Indian relatives?'

'No.'

'No Indian DNA?' he insists.

'Erm...no. Not that I know of.'

I'm pretty well-documented on this. My sister sent me her DNA test from Los Angeles. It appears we have a 5.1 per cent of British-Irish genes unaccounted for in the family tree. Which might explain my penchant for Guinness beer. But no, no Indian blood in my veins as far as the DNA test reveals.

'Are you sure?' he's relentless.

'Yes, as much as I can be, why?'

'Well, you have a very distinctive iris that is typical only of Indian people. I have many Western patients, but I have never seen in them this particular type of iris that only my Indian patients have. It is a typical Indian iris shape. If I hadn't seen that you're white, I would've sworn you're Indian.'

So that jocular law student, Somdev's girlfriend at the Cricket Club party, had been right all along: I *am* a reverse coconut! White on the outside, while the brown inside me is beginning to show through my eyes—only, you need a microscope to see it. I finally feel included.

Hospitals are the most cosmopolitan place you will find in Chennai. People travel all the way from West Bengal, from Gujarat, from as far away as the Gulf countries to get cured here, where you'll hear many Indian languages, Arab accents and run into the occasional European who wants to save money on a major surgery and take a plunge into the unknown.

I know Chennai hospitals because I've had it all.

The ailments, I mean.

Not really all, but a lot of issues that crop up when you inch towards your 50s, and also when you settle into a tropical life you weren't necessarily built for.

It all started at the Madras Boat Club, where my wife put me up when I first came back to visit her after our kiss in Venice. I was not introduced to her parents until later. I was being tested, I presume. So she stowed me there, while checking out my (and her) long term intentions. I guess we wisely thought we'd take our time.

The problem is that by the time I arrived in Chennai my stomach had been invaded by some revolutionary elements all bent on changing my intestinal flora.

My yoga-people mind at the time even tried to see that as some sort of Ayurvedic purification, letting go of deep-seated toxins in my stomach, puking them all out, when they weren't going down the other alley.

It took a lot of love to get through the vomiting and diarrhoea, those long days and sleepless nights, overlooking the Adyar River reeking with the smell of sewage and clouds of hungry mosquitos. I discovered Imodium and a list of Latin sounding medicines full of Xs and Ys, which it would be pedantic to roll out here.

Over the years, I discovered Chennai through its doctors.

Not just the lethargic Dr Ganesh who I'd catch napping on a cot taking an afternoon nap in his office; or Dr Anand, the marathon-running dermatologist who'd prescribe a muscle relaxant cream to cure my keratosis (it worked) and treat successfully my feet and toes for several skin issues; or the ophthalmologist who warned me to 'Always wear your coolers!' (which I discovered means 'sunglasses' in this archaic version of South Indian-English); or the ENT doctor who took a giant pump filled with warm water and sprayed it into my ear, washing out a strange fungus that had inhabited my head for months; or the gastroenterologist who, not making much progress with my stomach pains, in the end passed me on to his more Ayurvedically inclined daughter, who prescribed some equally ineffective homeopathic alternatives.

When I tried curing my chronic back-ache, Harri passed me on to his physiotherapist Murali ('I'm one of the few licensed chiropractors in India!').

He didn't tell me, but did tell Harri, that he thought my problem, aside from my classic lordosis and scoliosis, was not some newly blossoming sciatica pinching my nerve on a disc that an orthopaedic Chennai luminary was dying to substitute with prosthesis, but that I had 'done yoga all wrong'.

It was a common diagnosis he'd apply to many Western patients, I discovered.

How can the vellais know how to do yoga? They'll push too hard and hurt themselves. They don't have a body for it, right?

My Chennai doctors…I see their moustachioed faces run past my memory, as in a fast-forwarded dream.

Wearing their comfortable sneakers, those who studied in America, or sporting more elegant leather loafers, those who affected an English accent picked up at a British university, or those who went comfortably barefoot, just like any other local, and put some sandalwood paste on the image of a deity, in their incense-flavoured waiting rooms.

They fly past my mind's eye as in a speeding Instagram scroll: the audiogram technician who insisted that carrying out a hearing exam right below the excessively loud Adyar bridge flyover made total sense, because it was the normal noise I'd hear in most of India; the hearing aid technician who kept trying to fix my left ear instrument without ever managing to do it, but had good filter coffee, while I waited and observed the meticulous assembling work in the labs…

I began to enjoy discovering Chennai through its medical waiting rooms, a great place to make friends.

Getting cured or having your health looked into in this part of India is less scary than the sterile gaze of the Italian, American or British doctors I'd encountered before. There's something in the humanity of the process that already predisposes you towards healing. Maybe a less pervasive feeling of fear of death, as well? Could be.

It is not all just cells and chemicals, it can't be.

That touch of humanity I've experienced even with the busiest doctors in Chennai is central to the cure, maybe not as central as competence in your specialization, but I'm convinced it contributes to healing.

Hello? This is my irrational self speaking. I know that.

Yet this is the layman's opinion of someone who's also learned not to hope for fast cures, and to cohabit with pain.

It's part of the Vedic lesson learned in India. It's the same pain I keep feeling now in my hip, as I lean over the desk to write these very words.

For me, meeting a new health expert, a new yoga guru, a new luminary in my Indian years, has always been an experience in discovery, in drilling down deeply into the essence of the country.

The Ayurvedic alternative is always peeking through. Friends of all ages trust their Western medicine clinics, but will also pull oil in their mouth, put oil on their cranium, into their ears, follow grandma's advice. Because it works.

'It works if you believe in it,' a master sorceress once taught me in the Mountains of Northern Argentina. (There goes 'the most interesting man in the world' syndrome again. I had warned you.)

It may not have been confirmed by Western studies, but, hey, my ache gets better, so I keep doing it. And not just because it is tradition, nor because oil, paste and Ayurvedic concoctions are possibly made of chemicals which cure you just as well, and at times more cleanly, than Western chemicals. But because it just works, plain and simple.

So I go with both. But when the going gets really tough, I stoop to the occasional antibiotic, the 'anti-life' as the name indicates, the atomic bomb which kills the good with the bad, forcing you to build back your strength a lot more slowly.

Self-reliance as a most un-Indian quality

Or how to stay in your place to survive 'Bureaucrazy'

Understanding the mentality and fitting in a host culture, including the one I grew up in, has been my life's unspoken mission.

I've not lived here in India to only do my journalistic or authorial profession, to just write my books and articles, no matter what.

At the very foundation of the task of writing articles and books there has been the attempt to fit in, in order to understand how things work: mentally, socially, here, in such a distant culture. Many Westerners I've run into give up after a while.

Part of this process has happened inevitably with the deadly embrace of bureaucracy, or *burocrazy*, as they punnily call it here. I've had to face a particular bureaucratic challenge myself, as a mappillai in Chennai.

I could not ask for practical help from my dear father-in-law, since he's already taxed with the responsibility of managing the lives and affairs of many people in his family. He's the *paterfamilias*. His parents have both passed away and so has his beloved brother, swiped up by a cancer when he was still in middle age.

He's in charge of helping out his sisters and his sister-in-law, he's keeping accounting and fiscal tabs on his wife and both daughters. And he's also partially in charge of the daily tasks of his disabled son, Ajay, getting him through dinner, preparing him for bed.

Thus it became rather clear and only fair that the arrival in the household of yet another element, the mappillai, could not possibly add to the increasing list of *lafda-tamasha* (worries) that this generous man was already carrying on his strong shoulders.

All the while, by the way, keeping constant good humour, laughing in the face of the worst of worries, and always finding the chuckling side of things, in our long chats during the customary roti-dal-bhat-saak Gujarati dinners.

A real cheerful guru to be followed by example.

I owe him a lot. And love him dearly for it.

This is why I ventured out into the world of opening a bank account, buying a car, registering my marriage, getting a PAN card, renewing my visa, getting an AADHAAR card, surviving demonetization and learning about the new taxation system of GST mostly on my own.

My father-in-law's network could help up to a point, since he had an army of cousins and relatives to deal with. I had to prove my mettle. And face the Hydra-headed Indian bureaucracy mostly on my own.

This is why I found myself on the phone, screaming through my lungs at a bank official when my wire transfer did not come through while trying to buy a car before our wedding, and made it only a couple of months later, even though I'd been using the help of 'a fixer'.

You have to know, if you don't already know it, that middle class people in India often do everything through a fixer. I mean you can try by yourself. Keep calling. Keep showing up. Keep filling out the forms, keep cutting the line, keep going back day after day to the same office. Be patient. Insist kindly. Constantly. It'll take years off your life.

Or you can look for a fixer.

My wife's driver's licence needs renewal?

She calls Harri and asks for a fixer who can manage it.

I have to buy a car?

I ask Raghu to put me in touch with his fixer.

You need something done, you find a fixer.

He's not an accountant, nor a shady middle-man, but someone who, if needed, might find out when and if a bribe is necessary, but, mostly, it is a man or a woman who knows the process, knows which documents are required and where they have to be submitted.

There'll be a fee. Trust me, it's worth it.

You'd think it's an inefficient process, but within the Indian context it makes total sense.

See, this Anglo-Saxon self-reliance, this Protestant ethic which industrialized the American East, and also conquered and built the Wild West of America (while massacring hundreds of thousand of Native Americans who to this day still live in Reservations) doesn't cut it, here in India. It just ain't the thing.

In fact, there is something deeply un-Indian about self-reliance.

I spot it while observing Rohit, a Dilliwala friend, staying with us at the beach house. He's not aware, even for an instant, that since there's no house help to clear the table after he's savoured my famous tomato pasta, it would be appreciated if he contributed by bringing his own dirty plate back to the kitchen.

I mean, he doesn't have to wash it, God forbid. But at least spare me or my wife from having to bring his cutlery back to the sink. A non-Indianized mind might even take offence. I absolutely don't.

I know Rohit has been raised in a privileged Indian household, where you are really *not* supposed to bring your plate back to the kitchen. It would be an insult to your host. And, plus, it's not only an insult to your own role in family and society, it's an insult to the role of the person who is paid to live with you in order to clear your plate off the table.

There's always 'a guy' or 'a woman' for the job. You play your role, you follow your dharma and don't try to be too many things you're not supposed to be.

You're a photographer? Take photographs.

You're not a waiter who clears the table! There's someone for that.

This explains why you may find many successful, well-off Indian middle-aged men who'll tell you everything about BitCoin blockchain engineering or can explain the relationship between string theory and Vedic thought, or hedge-funds and developing nations, or…and on and on all the way to Tam-Bram heaven.

But they will not know how to operate a power-drill.

This self-reliant, do-it-yourself, I'm-my-own-cowboy thing is the most un-Indian thing you could be.

I know, because I come from the most self-reliant region of Italy.

One of the derogatory nicknames other Italians have for us Veneti is *'faso tuto mi'* which in Venetian means 'I will do it all myself', and this explains the obsession for opening your own little factory, being your own boss, and absolutely never stepping back if you've got to roll up your sleeves and get in the muck with your workers, proving you're one of them, that you have the same technical skills they have and you can do it just as well as they can.

This wins respect where I come from.

Here, I've attempted to contribute in transporting the Ganesh statue to the garden in Arlanymor. And I've ventured to assist the air conditioning installers with their ladders and tools.

And I've tried to give a hand to the family electrician by pulling on the right cable, participating in the analysis of the problem at hand. And I realize, as I witness their startled grimaces, that I'm breaking the caste rule. I'm not staying in my place.

'Ah, sir...' sighs the phlegmatic Logu, the sturdy electrician, as he attempts to jump on the kitchen counter to change the neon light tube.

While I hand him a screwdriver, he shakes his head in mild disapproval of my eagerness. But, by now, he's somewhat learned to live with this odd instinct of mine. And I've also learned to realize I'm embarrassing him.

The more down and dirty you get in the garden, the more you are demeaning the people who by definition should be there, getting down and dirty.

Somehow, I feel that by doing something that in their eyes is demeaning for your stature, you are demeaning their own role as your people, your assistants, the guys who are supposed to do that thing *for* you, not *with* you, for Chrissake!

But there's a deeper level to this. A political angle.

The *haves* hire the *have nots* for the smallest and easiest tasks, sometimes. This is something that at first seems unbearable to Americans who move to India without proper cultural training.

Once they get it (but they rarely truly get it, in the most specific way), they are those who behave most like slave-owners (something white Americans actually have a somewhat recent historical background in).

Or maybe it just stands out more, because of the colour of the skin.

For example, the American son-in-law of a Chennai friend of my wife, who at first abhorred the treatment of helpers and lower level fixers sent out late at night to buy that whimsical banana or milk, was the first one, once settled in, to send out the watchman to get him beers. Something the watchman certainly shouldn't do in alcohol-complicated Tamil Nadu.

The system of fixers and helpers who do simple, easy tasks you could do yourself is actually a way to distribute income.

It's not equal, but it's a way to keep social peace.

It's a way to share your wealth.

It is tacitly understood to be that, at least this is what it looks like to me.

It's a homeopathic cure to the glaring inequalities of life in the Socialist Republic of India.

Caste grumpiness

Or how to act in the dharmic movie of your life surrounded by extras

I'm sitting at the breakfast table, showing my back to the white wicker chairs in the sun-filled veranda by the narrow green lawn. Next to me, my father-in-law is merrily dipping away his khakhras, a thin, wheat flour cracker, in a bowl of curd, spicy pickles and sweet mango chutney—his Gujarati breakfast.

The rest of us go continental with a delicious home-made muesli, scrambled eggs, toast, coffee, sliced papaya and freshly squeezed orange juice—the simple yet energy-filled culinary bliss that starts our days in Chennai.

It's a hot March morning. My wife sits opposite me and my mother-in-law next to her. At the head of the table, there's an empty plate as Ajay, my brother-in-law, is the last one to join us. Everyone has to be seated before he takes his place. It's his thing.

Mosquitos are sinking their fastidious little pins into my calves and ankles.

'Kala is leaving,' my mother-in-law announces.

'What's happening?' my wife asks, startled to discover that one of the pillars of the regular daily household is pulling out. The live-in Dravidian maid and cook, Kala, is indeed leaving us, along with her two little girls.

'Did she get a better job? Did she find a new husband?' I ask, forever optimistic.

'If only!' my mother-in-law says.

My father-in-law begins to explain: 'Well, she's gotten mixed up in some money lending scheme...'

Turns out she was the one giving loans at high rates. She was not the borrower, but the lender. And things got complicated, as they often do in these contexts. Someone may be after her, she would not explain. All she could say is that she, and the two girls who occasionally ran around the house, would have to get going. And fast. Is it a true story or a complicated excuse for something else? Hard to tell.

Now we'd have to get by without help until we could find someone new. The word-of-mouth 'employment agency' made up of a network of friends and acquaintances would have to get jump-started.

Trials, interviews, tests, background checks would need to be done until a new member of the household could join us to alleviate household chores.

This is when someone you've become partially familiar with, although you are never really able to become familiar with them, suddenly disappears from your Indian life.

It's taken me years to absorb the intricacies of the relationship between so-called helpers and the people who pay their salaries. It cost me a lot to master this strange feeling of cohabiting with drivers, cleaners, cleaning ladies, cooks and watch-persons, allowing them to be there as the extras in the movie of our lives, the background people who take a tertiary role, who just move from room to room, appear and disappear and are not really ever fully acknowledged.

Tough, for someone with my background.

Kala was eventually substituted by the smiling young Kanchana. Thin and elegant, chipper and constantly jovial to make up for her initial lack of skills in the kitchen, which she slowly recovered from, under the caring gaze and teachings of my mother-in-law. She was not afraid to smile, which is not the simplest thing as we'll find out.

She didn't last long enough, as her father eventually discovered she had quit her job as a sales clerk in a shop and was 'working in a house'.

Kanchana's father felt this was below their caste's standards. And he was also afraid she'd elope with some boy who was buzzing around her.

So she was forced to quit her job and replaced by the somewhat grumpier Vadame. Older, weathered, and permanently saddened by the misadventures of an alcoholic son who kept getting into trouble by falling into a ditch or running into debt with shady characters.

She eventually cheered up some, but not much. Her country Tamil is so tight that many of the city people who interact with her seem to also have a hard time understanding her.

I stopped greeting her with a smile, because it seemed to almost scare her. I decided to just act like her. Practical, technical, hopping around the kitchen to avoid stepping on each other's toes. (Yes, I do make my own coffee or prance around the refrigerator at times. I'm self-reliant, remember?)

Equally grumpy is Nagama, the cleaner who rings the door bell in the afternoon to come wash the floors, sweep, mop the bathrooms. She trudges up and down the stairs with her stout hips and narrower shoulders, dragging behind her brooms and buckets. Efficient, down to the point, no time to waste. Stone-faced.

Again, my vellai smile is totally out of place, being met with a cold expression, as I quickly learned that my teeth baring is not welcome.

This is caste grumpiness I'm talking about. A wall of sour, yet indifferent distance which is put on not just by the Ammas and the Sirs, but also by the workers of the house towards the Ammas and the Sirs.

Smiles in Tamil Nadu have a different meaning from what I was accustomed to in the US or in Italy. Here, you often smile in front of pain, stress, confusion or after a risk you just survived, a fate you escaped. And yet, I take advantage of this cultural divide and bask in the pleasure of being surrounded by the sweetness of

Tamil smiles, uncaring whether or not they mean a sign of sympathy, courtesy or if they are a meaningless mask.

Interlude: A brief history (and science) of smiles

There's a whole science to the meaning of smiles across cultures.

People living in immigration-based countries like the US, Canada or Australia naturally smile more. These frontier societies, where initially there was more anarchy due to little presence of state authorities, developed the need to quickly signal to strangers the message: 'I am a friend. (Please don't shoot me!)'

And this is why there's such a thing as the appropriately named 'Pan-American Smile', the forced-polite wince of flight attendants—deadpan eyes, cheekbones pulled up to arch the corners of the mouth. You may call it also the Berlusconi, or Alligator smile, if it works better for you.

Quite different from what is known as the more likeable 'Duchenne Smile'—no teeth showing, cheekbones pulled, eyes squinting. Difficult to fake. Gotta be heartfelt. Think Clint Eastwood.

Then there's what could be called the Asian smile, with wide differences within that category, as we're talking about the most populated continent in the world with all its diversities. The Japanese smile is figuratively and literally thousands of miles apart from the Indian smile. The South Indian smile is quite different from the North Indian smile, too.

Compared to the Pan-American smile of the New Continent or the Duchenne smile of Europe indicating either courtesy or happiness, in many Asian societies people may also smile when they are embarrassed, angry, sad, confused, stressed, apologetic, and, of course, also when they're happy.

So you better look at the eyes, windows of the soul, instead of the mouth, to interpret the meaning of each smile, a technique many Japanese have learned to master quite well.

Smile seems to have sprouted in primates, according to scholar Frank McAndrew. It was discovered that baring teeth held together could be interpreted as a sign of submission, instead of the menacing open mouthed growl which meant: 'I will bite you, dude.' It means that if my teeth are together, I'm not ready to bite. Absence of threat as a sign of amicability.

In many non-immigrant based countries, like Russia, China or Japan, smile is often only for friends, not strangers. Chinese stewards at the Olympics were instructed to hold chopsticks in their mouths to train their little used Pan-American 'smiling muscles' before facing the international crowd.

Many traditional Russians are averse to smiling in public. As Maxim Gorky famously stated: 'The main thing you see in an American is teeth.' No wonder the Cold War lasted so long. Nowadays, however, in order to improve the country's public relations even the notoriously morose Russian border guards are instructed to smile more. And so are the famously unfriendly French tourist authorities.

The Japanese even have a specific word for a typical grimace—the 'naki-wari' is a smile to be employed to show anger, sadness or embarrassment. Koreans say 'He who smiles a lot is not a real man.' Ancient Romans said laughter abounds in the mouth of the fool.

Scientists have even compiled an entire chart showing how much individual cultures believe that smiling means you are either stupid or dishonest.

Smiles take on different meanings in different contexts. And definitely a different meaning is attached to baring teeth. Unhappy, stressed out by the rat-race Americans smile all the time. While unsmiling, hard-faced Swiss, Norwegians and Swedes are allegedly living in the happiest Western societies. Statistics indicate Germans value the importance of smiling more than any other European country and yet probably have one of the most inscrutable senses of humour in the continent.

What about India?

Indian brides are not supposed to smile as much as Western brides, it is believed, as Indian macho culture values female shyness, and a more serious expression is expected, almost demanded, or at least it's considered the norm until today.

This could explain why younger Kanchana, imbued by Western culture through TV and Internet had a happy-go-lucky grimace, while the more weathered, mature Nagama and Vadame give me the dropped cheek, eye-lids at half mast, no bullshit, frozen look.

Outspokenness and an extrovert attitude have not historically been very appreciated or rewarded in traditional Indian culture, and public speaking and communications skills have not been extremely encouraged either.

Some are even convinced that Indian life is such a cut-throat context that people around you in public spaces are considered your competitors, if not adversaries, so smiling can be interpreted either as a sign of weakness, a willingness to give in and submit, or as an indication of shady dishonesty.

In fact, India, Argentina and the Maldives associate public smiling to dishonesty more than other cultures, according to the Polish Academy of Science, and Japan, India and South Korea also associate happy smiling with less intelligent people.

Personally, I see a lot of smiles in the land of the Dravidians. I am actually impressed by the serenity and availability of smiles in South India, compared to the more challenged Indo-Aryan North. It may be connected to a healthier economy down here, but I just enjoy the benefits of the relaxedness it creates. And, yet, I have also grown aware of the fact that a smile does not mean you are not stressed.

Here in Chennai, I once watched a lady almost roll off a bus once, nearly breaking her neck. She managed not to fall to the ground and danced away on her feet with a big smile, where a Western counterpart would have been cursing away or at least grimacing in fear of having almost killed herself.

When I fastidiously pick on my wife, I see that her reaction is first of all a smile. Which my European upbringing interprets incorrectly as: 'Keep at it, it's fun.' It's not, really. I know. I just can't help it.

Again, I find it useful for any vellai to quickly read the memo on the different smiling code, a central technique to master in India.

The unknown Babu, Munni and Ammus of my daily life

There's nothing that will make Babu the driver smile. Well, maybe a very generous tip, like the one my mother gives him when she comes to visit in Chennai. That's the once-a-year occasion when Babu will finally let out a wide, long, slow smile.

Babu's in charge of driving Ajay, born with Down syndrome and who later developed autism, to his schoolwork every day. He walks Ajay to the car, helps him settle in and takes off into that traffic you have read all about in an earlier chapter.

Babu's got a '50s style full tuft of hair, drags his slippers around the garage, his every movement seems to slow down more and more, as years go by. He has basic knowledge of some English, but it's been almost impossible for me to ever have a full conversation with him.

Babu's also smashed up a couple of cars. Not totalled them, but I once was in a single ride with him when he managed to get two scrapes on the side of the car and one serious 'bum hit'. He goes through ups and downs. Family trouble, health trouble. Won't show up at the last moment, when you have to go to the airport in the morning, for example.

In a normal context, he'd be fired. But this is the other side of the medal of the so-called 'Indian private welfare system', and so if you are a decent, big-hearted person like my father-in-law, you don't fire someone because they go through a rough patch. You pay for them to be visited by a private doctor, if necessary. It may be to unmask white lies about his condition, or it may be to give him proper help.

Who knows? This is India, contradictions everywhere, remember?

Babu stays. Grumpy as a grouch can be, not really

efficient, pumping up and down on that pedal so you can get appropriately car sick. But he stays. There's some sort of security within this system, however flawed. Where meritocracy meets humanity, perhaps?

I am most intrigued and fond of Munni, the Dravidian painter who's a founding pillar of the family I married into, although he's technically at the bottom of the scale.

He sleeps on the floor of the garage, something I found unbearable to think about for months. Well, a couple of years actually. But he doesn't seem to care, as difficult as that is for me to accept.

He opens and locks the gate in the morning and at night, does some carpentry work, and most of all he's specialized in painting houses and buildings, having some carpentry skills too, as he also takes on jobs in the neighbourhood.

I've gone to buy gardening tools with him or driven him to the shop, and yet I feel that even if my Tamil were better there wouldn't be room, socially, for a real discussion between the two of us.

As I lay in bed in the guest bedroom, right above the garage where he sleeps, I often wonder about his life right below me. And I try to quell my feeling of misplaced pity.

I admire his seriousness, his dignity, what looks like the rust-proof sturdiness of his vegetarian morality, a devout Hindu without any excesses of religious pride or iconography, zero judgement in his eyes when my wife and I get back to the house slightly tipsy, sometimes, late at night. He does affect what seems like a real smile— mild, serene, wise, or so it seems to my eyes.

He's there, solid, reliable, yet proud or, rather, dignified. I know it's a vellai cliché, this admiration of 'dignified poverty in India', but I embrace it, just this one time.

There's nothing inferior about him. I'd say there's something superior, in fact, but that would be my Western mind finding too much poetry in inequality.

I do want to get a translator and sit down to talk to Munni for hours, find out about his son who got married, and shows up here once in a while, already looking so different from his father, so much more modern, glued to his phone screen as he is.

I'd like to know about Munni's village where he goes regularly to tend his fields. The incurable whitey would like to know more of the life of this person. And yet the reverse coconut in me knows I can't do that.

I would also like to know why Ammu never smiles when she's photographed by the many guests who visit my wife and me in Arlanymor. She's all smiles the rest of the time, but click it and those teeth will disappear almost mechanically, as if programmed by an AI application on your smartphone.

Ammu and Sampath are the handsome couple who look after the property by living here in Arlanymor. They have two sons, 12 and 13 years old. Ammu makes sure they go to good schools. One of them is a Christian, the other a Hindu. She's got her religious options covered in a traditionally ecumenical way.

One afternoon, I caught one of these well-educated boys pissing in the driveway. Again, cultural context. Doesn't mean he was doing it to deface the employer's home. Does it?

Ammu, the brighter of the couple, is a 29-year-old Dravidian lady with a smile that'll warm your heart as she flashes that ivory feast of her fully toothed grin in front of everything. No matter if she's being femalesplained by my wife that she once again forgot to do something or other. She'll giggle happily right through it, a candid rave party dancing in her mouth.

Once, while picking mussels out of the sand at the beach with my mother, she started showing off some yoga moves. She's now got a big flat screen TV at her parents' house, a couple of km from Arlanymor, in the west-facing Paramankeni hamlet. She learns all the moves from a TV guru, possibly the lean and controversial Baba Ramdev.

She's a constant presence in the house. 'Saaaahr...' she yells, breaking my mid-morning writing sprees. During our co-habitation her English has improved impressively, compared to my non-existent progress in Tamil: 'Sir, going to hospital, coming back three'; 'Going to school, teachers parents meet, coming back four'; 'Going to village, market, back 2:30!'; 'Going pay bill'; 'Going bank'; 'Sampath uncle heart attack, going hospital'; and so on.

She feels the need to create a different story every time, even though no one expects her to be here the whole day, anyway. Class dynamics I don't dare to interfere with.

Most of the time, Ammu keeps busy washing the dishes, watering the lawn, cleaning the porch. With her and my mom, we do pooja offerings together at the Ganesh statue once or twice a year, at least. Then she takes us to honour the spirit God that was here before that Ganesh statue, a simple short tree on the path out to the beach.

She's always elegantly clad in her bright coloured sari, at times stopping to inhale the fragrance of the frangipani, while watering the new palm saplings out there in the large vegetable garden.

I'm used to her. She seems very familiar by now.

And, yet, when she slips while mopping the floor downstairs, while I'm upstairs writing, and I hear her scream, once I reach her and ask her to come and sit on the chair, rest, recover, let me look at her wrist, she's reluctant.

She will not sit on the chair. She'll sit on the floor. I can only gather that she would consider it an insult to my role, but also to her role, if she sat on the chair where I dine every day.

It's not her place, the message seems to be. And when I go and get her a glass of water, she says 'no', and points to the metal cup, and I have to go back and get her the cup she uses for her tea. But I'm appalled at all this, at this custom, which I'm seeing she is enforcing, not me.

But she won't drink from our glasses. And I know all that is behind it—the caste system, the divisions, but I don't want it. It is Ammu who seems bent on enforcing it, her reaction a result of centuries of oppression and conditioning ingrained in the culture she grew up with.

I can't help but think it must look eccentrically unfair to her eyes, spending all this money on dog food. Spoilt people, really.

While she picks up the thin leaves of grass I broadcast all around me with a brand new string brush cutter. I also cannot help but think of what could be her internal monologue which might be something like this: 'What the hell is wrong with these people? I have to water this lawn every day, so that it grows lush and green. Then they buy an expensive contraption to cut it down, spend more money on petrol and oil to mow down the grass, so that it looks burnt and yellow again, because of the shadow from the long green grass that was just cut. All so that I may start to water it back again, so it grows back and then they can cut it and make it yellow once again. Wasting petrol. And water. Plus they are not feeding this luxury grass to any animal, they are having me throw it away!'

Who am I to Ammu's eyes? A stupid vellai, I fear.

But who is she? Who is Sampath, her typhoid-prone husband? I really don't know. And never would I have thought I'd be able to live so close to someone, and yet ignore who they really are, what they really are like.

The journalist, the writer, the human being would want to know more. The dreamer who wanted to write about the weak, the poor, the downtrodden so that more equality can come about, stands defeated in his golden paradise at the beach.

The vellai mappillai knows that in order to belong here, he can't satisfy that thirst.

I have to accept how things are here. They are different from what I had imagined.

We live near each other, the 'extras' and us, and we do not really connect humanly, at a deep level. And this probably spares us a lot of troublesome complications that I see peeking through a request for a loan which then turns into a complicated monetary relationship of dependence and bondage.

What would my past self of 2008 say about this present, apparently jaded self of 2018? He might not like this aspect of my current integration.

He might not get it.

Ammu is at the door again. She wants to talk to my father-in-law who is visiting for the weekend. She needs to borrow some money again. It will be subtracted from her salary, in installed payments, over the next nine months.

She's fine with it. She can take it. She's most likely the only one of her enlarged family who has an employer from the big city; she's the relative with access to the possibility of borrowing without falling prey to loan sharks and their dangerous consequences.

And again, the reason for the loan is almost always the same—a wedding in the family.

You may understandably judge this as a waste of resources, constantly living in debt to finance weddings for all family members, where instead you could invest in improving your condition more permanently. But, if you live here, you have to concede that there is a cultural, contextual need for this. A flashy wedding is actually about guaranteeing you can maintain your social condition.

This is the country where the way your wedding plays out is representative of how you are regarded in society. It can be a long term investment in the family prestige; a guarantee you can stay, and possibly climb up in reputation, within your caste.

Although I know it doesn't make much sense anywhere else, but splurging money for a wedding is cash well spent in this Indian context. Better than throwing it away on processed dog food!

I know first hand about the pivotal importance of the marriage ceremony, here, as I got myself offered a big fat Jain Scottish Welsh Venetian Indian Wedding!

HERE COMES THE GROOM:
LOVE AND MARRIAGE GO TOGETHER
LIKE BULLOCKS AND CARRIAGE

Being taught there's only one fool at a wedding, pointing to male chauvinistic stars, being told I can't hold hands and contemplating the mysteries of married life in THE FUTURE OF INDIA.

My big fat Jain-Scottish-Welsh-Venetian-Indian Wedding

There is only one fool at every marriage ceremony: the groom

> There was a young maid from Madras
> Who had a magnificent ass;
> Not rounded and pink,
> As you probably think—
> It was grey, had long ears,
> and ate grass.
> —Adult Limerick

It was on 4 January 2014 when for the very first time in my life I found myself trying not to fall off a cart pulled by two giant water buffalos.

That's right, I was not riding a regal white horse, nor was I perched astride a majestic elephant, as I had originally asked, but...bullocks! I mean, literally.

Ok, the cart, or matavandi, had been freshly painted and adorned in bright, festive colours. The buffaloes sported two Pongal-style pink and magenta horns and the conductor's white turban and new lungi competed with my golden kurta and bright orange turban.

From up there in the *matavandi*, it felt very much like Games without Borders, the TV competition I'd watch enthusiastically as a child, pitting nation against nation in a European-wide TV show.

The bridegroom's team was donning orange turbans; the bride's relatives were sporting pink ones. The bridegroom team had no idea what it was doing, but luckily two generous cousins, Pankaj and Kunal, betrayed their ranks to instruct the vellais on how to play their part in the ceremony.

I had gathered my cosmopolitan tribe. There were a lot of dear, lifelong friends from my hometown Valdagno, Tania, Elisa, Nicola, Luca, Sara, who on that trip got renamed 'Wild-agno' in honour of the wild times, or maybe of the Wildlings, the Free Folks of *Game of Thrones*, as this is what the rustic folks from my valley must look like to the more refined people of the Venetian plains.

There were some friends from London, New York, Naples and Rome, friends met in Mexico, my mother, my sisters and their children. We were ready to take on the town. And the countryside.

Make no mistake, my wife and I were fully aware that marriage ceremonies are puppet acts in which bride and groom are there to provide entertainment for family and friends.

The betrothed are not the real focus of the party.

The real focus are the guests, the relatives, the public of that pantomime.

Marriage is scientifically proven to be the main cause for divorce, yet having an Indian wedding provides a greater antidote against divorce: who's got the energy to ever repeat such a torturous process?

This is what I was thinking about, as I wobbled along, dragged by the two colourful buffalos, while my wedding army was instructed to chant in Hindi: 'Here comes Carlo the King!'

Although I rather think I looked more like an overdressed buffoon, up there in my unlikely cultural-appropriation of a turban, for a second I did picture myself as that King coming to get his Queen. *Oh, Narcissus, how I love thee! I believe in a reign called Carlo Pizzati, I'm the number one patriot of Carlolandia!*

Little did I know the ceremony is a game played on several levels, where 'the conquering army of the groom' is duped into believing it is coming to whisk the bride away, only to be ensnared into the spires of the hosting bride's family. Which, in this case, was bound to triumph.

Isn't this the perfect allegory of most marriages?

As we approached the house, all the slow pitfalls became clear.

There were several symbolic games to be played. One of them was that my best man Fabrizio had to protect me from my mother-in-law, who was supposed to grab my nose.

This must have looked quite odd to the Italians, considering that in the language of Dante, to 'catch someone by the nose' means to make a fool of him.

And as Lorenzo, my brother-in-law, had reminded me many years before when he married my sister Editta: 'There's only one *bischero*, only one fool, at a wedding.'

Yes, you guessed it: the groom.

So my nose was caught and then Peter, my half-Japanese half-Belgian giant of a friend, hoisted me on his shoulders while the strongest cousin provided support for Tishani, as we jousted in the garland game.

This, I was told, is a way of establishing who will rule in the house, whether it is the husband or the wife. The spouse who first drapes the other one's neck with a marigold and jasmine garland will be the boss.

I slyly pretended for a couple of seconds to overpower my betrothed only to bow in submission and be festooned by my wedding garland which still hangs, alongside my wife's, in our bedroom.

Finally we reached the wedding stage draped in a baldaquin, where we sat down with our parents.

My future in-laws were sitting on Tishani's side, while on my side there was my mother, alone.

In 1993, my father had stopped talking to me, my mother, and my three siblings for no understandable reason except that while divorcing my mother he had opted to get rid of the whole burden of the family he had created.

Although he's now passed away, my father keeps living within me like a non-lethal incurable disease.

Could be the reason why my first novel is about a patricide. Perhaps. Enough said about his absence there. Let us not allow him to spoil the party.

As the preacher admonished me to 'be a good boy' in my marriage (yes, he said that to a 48-year-old man), and while my father-in-law, for the first time in four years of knowing me, showed a menacing side, almost threatening me up close to make sure I took care of his daughter (subtext seemed to me: 'If you ever leave her, there will be consequences!'), and my mom looked slightly disorientated by what I thought she might have found to be a bit too much of a *pagliacciata*—a clownery of overdressed, over-coloured, etno-chic weirdos—I was asked to choose a friend in the audience who'd come and perform one of the functions of the long ceremony.

This is where something very strange happened. I was told that the person I would pick for the next ritual would get married by the end of the year.

So I pointed towards my nephew Colin. He had been in a steady relationship with a sexy Ivorian-Belgian lady, Jutta, and I was convinced they would get engaged any day.

But Colin, bashful and shy like his mother, my dear sister Maya, skilfully dodged my index finger, pretending I was pointing to someone behind him, a much beloved long time friend who I'd met in New York in the late '80s.

But Carlo Vutera, also known by his stage name as

Carlo Montecarlo, a powerful and intense tenor who I'd warned and begged not to sing any Italian opera in order to avoid the caricature of Italians at a wedding, had been one of the most successful playboys I'd ever met.

He would never get married by the end of the year! He was allergic to it. He was without a doubt the 'least likely to get married bachelor' at any wedding.

Yes, you can imagine how this specific story is going to end.

Colin, who dodged coming to my wedding altar, broke up irreversibly with Jutta within months, while Carlo, who joined us, up there on the ritual stage, startling every single one of his friends, actually did get married before the end of the year to a lovely Cuban-American lady!

Watch out what you wish for in India, the superstitious yoga-people vellais always say.

But later Carlo Montecarlo had another surprise in store for us.

*

This whole Arya Samaj wedding process spared me from changing my name to Harsh Sadhaka and allowed me to retain Carlo Pizzati, although Tishani would love for me to add my mother's better sounding last name of Dal Lago, as in Carlo Pizzati Dal Lago.

I was also fine with all the Indian contradictions

contained in the 'Vaidika Marriage Ceremonial' booklet. First among many, the fact that it was sold to me for 100 rupees, although the price on the back cover says 50 rupees. Vellai prices, sir.

'"Marry the person you love" is the slogan of the Western culture. "Love the person you marry" is the command of the Veda.'

Udayavir Vedalankar, 'popularly known as VIRAJ', is the author of such booklet which tackles the thorny issue of arranged marriage, about which I have an unpopular opinion which I'll explain soon.

'It does not mean,' VIRAJ explains, 'that a person should marry a spouse he or she dislikes or even hates.'

No, indeed, you don't have to marry someone you hate…

Western friends will laugh at this, some Indian friends will put on a sad face, knowing way too many people in that situation, I mean way from the start of married life.

'Marriage should be arranged by parents and well-wishers of the prospective bride and the bridegroom, but must be approved by the bride and the bridegroom.'

I know this is difficult to take for 'the Western mind', whatever that may be, if it even exists. But, nowadays, how many in the West are letting an algorithm help them select their future spouse? That's modern and acceptable. Scientific. Allowing parents and 'well-wishers', whatever that comprises, to chip-in is frowned upon.

Let's stop to consider what the wedding booklet said next: 'There are hundreds of instances, where intense love evaporated within a few years after marriage. Where to love a married spouse is considered a sacred duty, such a tragedy is less likely to occur.'

Ok, not modern at all. I know.

This means you have to sacrifice your emotions in order to respect a contract decided by parents and, you guessed it right, 'well-wishers'. Hard to swallow.

But try to take a more ecumenical approach and consider it is often true that the fire that lights up in a flash goes out in a flash—falling in love is not equivalent to love.

Desiring someone physically with all your being doesn't mean you will be able to spend your life with them. Proven, tested, guaranteed.

So, there is something to be said in favour of certain aspects of arranged marriages. There's something to be said against the hallucination of modern love, as it has developed since the French Revolution, thanks to the artsy courtesans who were able to get the enamoured noblemen to marry them, as socially inconvenient as it was at the time—this is historically how love marriages became more widespread in Europe and later in America, which propagated the concept elsewhere.

Before that, passionate love rarely ended in marriage. Think of Romeo killing himself over Juliet in Montecchio

(Montague), half an hour away from the town where I grew up, so I know what I'm talking about.

Let's not forget that on the topic of love Italians can claim the lineage and expertise of the likes of Gian Giacomo Casanova, Lorenzo da Ponte (the librettist for *Don Giovanni*), Rodolfo Valentino and Marcello Mastroianni, just to name a few.

And yet, of course, love should know no boundaries. There should be no prohibitions against marriage between people who love each other. There should be no regards for differences of gender, caste, class, race or nationality. Obviously. I think most republican and democratic constitutions actually guarantee this, and in no way do I argue against that. I defend it, rather.

But coming from an overly romantic country of constantly fighting Italian families, and having lived for 11 years in the country with the longest standing highest divorce rate in the world (if you don't count the Maldives and Belarus)—America—I see some wisdom in using your mind, not only your heart when choosing a spouse.

It makes sense to seek help from people who love you to get honest advice about real compatibility between you and the person you want to marry. And I think it is wise to profoundly consider what is being said to you, before deciding to get married.

I did not apply this logic with the person I chose to have a son with, a long time before getting married to

Tishani. And I made a mistake in that instinctive choice, pushed as I was by the irrational, not influenced in the least by the rather obvious rationale, in that context, which would have suggested I run from that situation which luckily resulted in a wonderful and adorable son.

It seems possible to me to strive for both the push of romantic love, accompanied by the analysis of compatibility in the long run between two people. The irresistible impulse, hand in hand with some reasoning about the long term plan.

When the high flames die out, you better be friends, if you want to survive the storm of time.

Equality might help. But in this, the 'Vaidika Marriage Ceremonial' booklet was also more optimistic than what I normally witness: 'In a marriage, man and women have equal status. A husband owns his wife; the wife owns her husband…A husband is the king as well as servant of his wife; a wife is the queen as well as maid servant of her husband. If they realise it, they will always be happy.'

And although the cover of the booklet warns that the marriage ceremony is the most important and elaborate, on page 10 it already tells you that 'marriage should be simple'. In India?

Nothing simple about the ritual that was going on under that canopy, in the garden of Arlanymor, while my wife and I circled the fire seven times, pouring ghee and chucking twigs into the flames, reciting mantras in Sanskrit which contained yet again some contradictions from that written promise of equality.

After getting water sprinkled on our heads, and looking into the sun, we repeated some very poetic words such as 'may we be able to see that eye, which has been placed in the sky by the divinities to observe the world, the sun rising before us in all its brilliance for a hundred autumns'.

Then we recited:

'May we live for a hundred autumns...'

Although why put a limit?

'May we hear clearly for a hundred autumns...'

Although I'd already been wearing hearing aids for a few autumns...

'May our speech remain clear and resonant for a hundred autumns...'

Although we were certainly mispronouncing most of these Sanskrit lines...

'May we remain undistressed [sic] and unrepressed for a hundred autumns...'

Again, make that 'forever', please...

'And if all these conditions prevail, may we live even for more than a hundred autumns...'

Ah, there you go!

But then comes that much disputed passage which some contemporary feminists have a problem with, understandably. Because the bridegroom will show the bride the Arundhati star, and she'll have to say:

'You are Arundhati, the un-restrainable, but I, Tishani, have been restrained by my husband Carlo,' which she repeated, although I'm not so sure she enjoyed that underlying pact of subjugation.

Weren't we supposed to be equal, as the initial axiom asserted?

But who cares? We were wearing our shiny Indian clothes, in this memorable afternoon, fire at our feet, a slight drizzle swiftly dried by the wind.

Sun, then clouds, and sun again.

Fire, water, air, earth, all the elements are here, and I think to myself in my spiritual atheist-cum-animistic mind:

'All the gods are here today.'

I looked over at the Ganesh statue and I couldn't help falling into a memory, thinking back of a *pradakshina*, a mantra-humming 14 km barefoot march around the holy mountain of Arunachala in the autumn of 2008, six years ago.

I was stomping along with a throng of 100 Italian Hindu pilgrims living for a month in a Tiruvannamalai ashram, deepening our practice of meditation.

During our circumambulation of the sacred mountain, considered to be the body of Shiva sprouting Shiva Lingams everywhere, we finally reached a quite important Ganesh temple.

Our teacher, Sergio, told us that if we kept asking in our mind a specific boon to Ganesh, as we crawled across the insides of its statue in an extremely narrow tunnel, that wish would soon be granted.

In that moment I thought that the whole point of Hindu philosophy was to free yourself of desire, and thus of the need to ask for boons, so I felt it was a trick question, as there should be nothing to ask, nothing to be desired.

I enquired, honestly within myself if I had reached that contentment, that holy Santosha that is gained by truly not having any needs. And, honestly, I could not say I had.

I was not happy, was I? Not really.

So I decided I'd ask Ganesh for nothing in specific, no focused goal, boon, wealth or materialistic gain. As I inched into that dirty, claustrophobic, narrow passage within that giant rock representing Lord Vinayak, the elephant-headed deity who puts and removes obstacles, I asked him to bring me some happiness and serenity.

'I just want to be serene, Ganesh,' is the only thought I repeated mentally, until I finally reached the light again, my white kurta all soiled by the tunnel crawl.

After leaving the Arunachala ashram, heading to Chennai in that distant 2008, it may be or may not have been a coincidence that the first new person I met was the woman who was now standing next to me on a wedding ceremony baldaquin on the Bay of Bengal, lighting the fire, walking around it, looking in the sun and in the un-restrainable star reciting mantras, while a rambunctious scuffle erupted among relatives and friends.

Part of the complex Gujarati marriage ceremony included also the fact that I would leave my slippers by the side of the stage and my two rather athletic sisters would be in charge of preventing the bride's family from stealing them.

I had forgotten to explain to my warrior sisters, made of strong moral and physical metal, that it was more of a ritual, not a game that we had to win at all costs. It was not Games without Borders, although it most certainly looked liked it. But us Wildlings from the dolomitic valleys are renowned for being competitive and fierce at protecting our property.

So Maya and Editta were clenching those gilded slippers with all their might, putting my acquired vegetarian Jain cousins into serious difficulty, causing a rugby tussle, toppling over cushions and chairs in the general laughter and bringing us back down from the heavens of spiritual remembrances and mystical contemplation of what our bond would mean, down to the earthy fact that this was supposed to also be FUN!

And fun it was, especially when my robust sisters stomped on the stage for the next ritual, which gives the name to the expression 'tying of the knot'.

It comes from the matrimonial gesture in which the groom's siblings have to come up to the altar and tie one end of the groom's scarf to the end of the bride's sari.

The problem is, again, that my Venetian sisters are all about being efficient, and determined to complete any task at their best. We sort of had a Prussian upbringing, in the shadows of the Alps, at the former border with Austria.

So Editta actually managed to tie such a strong knot, using a lot of my golden scarf, that not only was it impossible to untie (okay, good omen), but I almost got choked while she pulled, making me cough for help (bad omen).

The mantras and rituals were finally over and it all ended in a marvellous red petals' shower, which in my cheeseball mind I could not help but associate with the flowers that fell from the pergola in a restaurant on the banks of the Po River in Turin, four years before, in the first lunch Tishani and I ever had together, when we found that the cascading petals were just about too much, and walked away.

Dinner had its surprises as well. The Jain family had their own large round table, next to the Jain chef's counter, away from the un-Jain food which the 100 invitees started sticking their forks and knives and finger into, while some entertainment was provided.

First, our god-child Milo Zigi, age three, already

musically bent on becoming a rock star, sang 'Lucy and the Sky of Diamonds' a cappella.

Then, my percussionist friend Luca Nardon played along with Peter who strummed an Elvis tune on his guitar. Peter likes to wear fake sideburns and go 'Bebop-a-loolah', a remnant of his ancient busker days in Bruxelles before buying a castle near Paris.

And Editta, who's a Mozartian-voiced soprano, had prepared a duet with Carlo Montecarlo in honour of our house, to sing 'Arlanymor'.

There's such a song, in Welsh, which croons of that '*Ar Lan y Môr*', that place 'Beside the sea' where 'red roses are growing' (and I've been able to make them grow), where 'white lilies are showing' (and we've got white frangipani trees), where the beauty of these flowers is telling, and where 'my true love sleeps within her dwelling', where 'stones lie scattered', where 'tender words in love were uttered, while all around there grew the lily and sweetest branches of rosemary'.

But in Welsh, it all sounds like this: '*Ar lan y môr mae rhosys cochion, Ar lan y môr mae lilis gwynion, Ar lan y môr mae 'nghariad inne.*'

You see, not the easiest sounds to pronounce for two Italian opera singers.

They were managing just fine, until my sister squawked out a high pitch sound which the Welsh 'girls '—my mother-in-law's sister and her childhood friends—did not seem to recognize as properly Welsh.

As Editta kept coughing, we realized, as she explained later, that a mosquito had flown right into her open throat and got stuck there putting an end to this tearful, nostalgic song.

Then, as Fabrizio was droning on a passionate and ironic speech about our friendship and my love for Tishani, the electricity went off. Current gone!

It all fell into darkness, out there, beside the sea.

We suddenly heard the slow breathing of the ocean and waited for a generator to kick in. Which didn't.

From the corner of my eye, I saw Carlo Montecarlo jump to his feet.

No, I thought, *he's not going to do it.*

I warned him not to do it.

He better not do it.

'*O Soooooooooleeeee mioooooooo, sta in froooonte a teeeeeeee, o chistoooo sooooooooole…*'

Yes, he was doing it.

A capella, no music, in the darkness, to the awe of all our friends and family, he delivered the most heartfelt and most heartbreaking '*O Sole Mio*' I've ever heard, a song about the sun, about light, about love shining like a bright sun, right there in that seaside darkness, current gone, generator off.

And when he hit his final line, '*sta in froooooonote a teeeeeee!*' along with the roar of a very loud and long applause, the light magically came back and the dances started. Power back!

This is when it was time to establish a very simple fact called the dancing superiority of Indians. Although the 'Vaidika Marriage Ceremonial' prescribed or rather intimated: 'Tobacco is poison and wine is worse than tobacco. Both should be strictly prohibited at any Vaidika marriage.' And it also ordered that 'no one wants the night long marriage ceremonial', we had to break a couple of those rules.

Simply put, although Italians are acceptable dancers within the vellai category and have some sense of rhythm (think John Travolta now), there's something to be said here about Indians' relationship with their bodies when dancing, compared to Western rigidity. One word to the wise: the Bollywood shoulder roll.

One more thing I love about my wife is that wherever she is, if there's dancing music, she will dance.

So, if you're at that Notting Hill party which is not taking off on the dance floor and someone flips on a tune with some beat, she'll be the one who'll walk out there in the empty floor and swing it and hop it and smile and dance along. A proud ambassador of Indian dancing glee. She made me make so much progress with my small town Wild-agno self-consciousness.

And here they are, my new relatives, my Jain cousins and uncles and aunties, no embarrassment, no timidity, dishing out, with their moves, this useful lesson about life. Live it. Dance it.

I had to admit, as I watch them, that my Jain uncles, the ones who have already hit the big 60 mark, were killing it! They were out-dancing just about everyone with their smooth shoulder rolls, their elbows bouncing up in the air, their smile and distant gaze, the rapture, the irony, the cool.

But here came the kilts, as my acquired Scottish uncle waltzed in to his bagpipe tune, appropriately slipped on the Mp3 player by the DJ. It was time for the Celts to show their stuff and here they went, hoppity clogging away, as Vinod, my father-in-law who'd been going at this for most of his married life, joined in with some great moves, as my Wild-agno posse did what they do best, representing the valley with the proudly highest alcoholic rate within the region with the highest alcoholic rate in Italy: they drank it and they could take it. They'd even brought our town's favourite rotgut, Biancorosso, and we cheerily broke the Vaidika Marriage Ceremonial rules, while one of the vellai guests also did the Western boy and an Eastern girl thing and ended up getting laid, somewhere into the night.

Being married in India

So far so good, so far so good, so far so good,
so far so good

Marry the person you love. Love the person you marry.
Easily said.

My take on married life, or on life in general, for that
matter, is briefly summarized by this image I have of a
guy falling off a very high cliff and continuously saying
to himself: 'So far, so good, so far, so good…'

Everything ends. You never know when. No point in
delving into timing. Enjoy while you have it.

The impermanence of things. Lots of life's disasters
are caused by expectations, reflections of dreams on a
smoke-screen. Savour what you've got.

One of my favourite compositions written by my
wife is titled 'Love Poem'. It's the opposite of what you
may think by reading the title.

It's a woman talking to her lover as she tousles his
hair, while his head is lying on her lap. And she tells him
that everything ends, so why not end this now, before
we enter into the regret of a dead love. It's brilliant,
touching, true.

I mean, I do not see the point of jumping the gun,
but I get the point. I hope it never happens to me. But
things will eventually end. One way or another. It's just

that you don't want that future sadness to enter into your present serenity ahead of time.

*

The life of a long marriage. The wife looking across the table at the husband, slurping away his breakfast, hunched over his plate, digging his hand into his favourite dish, prepared in exactly the same way every single morning. She can't really hide her aggressive impulses, which he absorbs passively, knowing they won't amount to anything, like the distant lightning of a storm that will never hit land.

She's trying to hang on to the reasons why she loved him. She sees behind his slow rusting into a routine, which is closing him off from the outside world. She knows there's that wise man with a sense of humour, somewhere there, inside that husband, always ready for a laugh. She hangs on to that image in order to continue making breakfast every morning.

The long haul. It's a tough one.

Love and marriage. Horse and carriage. Or bullocks and carriage, to keep it Tamil.

It's weird being married in India, and it can sometimes be weird being married to an Indian woman.

In Italy, our obviously racially mixed marriage produces a corresponding rainbow of reactions. In their occasional racism, Italians often don't consider I may be married to a woman equally educated, equally smart, more successful, cosmopolitan, and worldly than they are. At first sight, some think I am the white man who went to rescue the lovely savage girl from that savage world. I know this for sure.

Men think: luccckyyyy. Women think: weak. Sometimes they ask me if I'm not one of those Western men who, fatigued by the aggressive, argumentative nature of the relationship with some Western women, went to look for a meek Asian bride.

None of them think of the possibility that I am generously being invited to live in my wife's house, with the contribution of my equally generous in-laws. No one ventures into the theory that I maybe the meek European groom, treated lovingly by not only a family, but in general by a welcoming, open-arms India.

Plus, they have no darned idea of the deserved reputation of Indian women.

My dear friend Nico from Wild-agno has already painfully split up with the delightful and fun woman he was with at my wedding. Now he's going through a crush for Nirmal, an attractive Punjabi devilish seducer from Delhi. I introduced them so I feel partially responsible for the trouble that is so obviously about to start. But Nico is really falling head over heels.

So I try to warn him.

Nico: 'I mean, we were on the couch and I was tired,

falling asleep, and she protectively pulled the blanket over my shoulders...you know what I mean? One of those gestures that makes you feel at home. Loved.'

Me: 'I see...Nico, be careful. This is a master operator. I'm not saying she doesn't enjoy the affair. I'm just saying: be careful.'

Nico: 'Why? What's wrong?'

Me: 'You know, one thing my wife once told me is that Indian women are like Italian men. Don't forget it.' (Think of the aforementioned Casanova, Valentino, Don Giovanni, John Travolta, Marcello Mastroianni tropes and you'll see what I mean.)

Nico: 'Wait, let me see, "Indian women are like Italian men..." Oh...Ah...no, wait, that's not good, is it?'

No, it's not. Keep your guard up. Don't be stupid. Don't be provincial. Don't fall into the clichés built in your mind. Get a spell-check for your brain!

It feels so weird to me, in New York, or London, or Venice or Wild-agno and sometimes here in India, when I hear things like: 'You, as a mixed couple...' or 'You, as a white man married to a woman of colour...'; I suppose bi-color is the new politically correct definition.

These things make absolutely no sense to me. They seem like something belonging to the end of an era which should long be over. I don't mean to advertise any United Colours of Benetton easy philosophy, but all these taxonomies...they make no sense. Although they are real, apparent, obvious, I do realize that.

But that's not the only cultural obstacle that hybrids can fall into.

Sometimes it takes a while to get accustomed to regular behaviour. Like walking down the street. Or strolling down Phoenix Shopping Mall, one of the few places in Chennai where you can walk miles up and down with air conditioning. As I reach for my wife's hand, she waves me away like a Melania with a Donald, and whispers, all in one breath: 'No PDA, no PDA, no PDA, remember? We're back in India now.' Bum-mmmerrr!

Anyone can rub on every inch of your body in an overcrowded train or bus, you get to feel uncles' bellies rubbed against your back, elbows, hips in every possible queue without the flinching of an eye, yet if a boy holds a girl's hands, some people start to bring out the knives. You can see wet t-shirt contests in Bollywood flicks, but try that in real life and you might get lynched. Indian contradictions are here, and are here to stay!

No PDA. This acronym was first used in some American campuses to prohibit shows of affection among lovers. What happened is that in the late 1960s universities began accepting co-ed dormitories. Colleges were supposed to act in *loco parentis*.

Some bigoted student at the University of Kansas in 1967 denounced the prevalence of PDA at the McCollum co-ed dorm and colleges stepped up an anti-PDA policy that has gone through ups and downs until today.

Usually PDA is an indication of a healthy relationship between two lovers, but these indications are not always perceived as healthy by others.

Something unbecoming of any puritanical culture. Fundamentalism, that's what it is. And my wife and I are submitting to it. Simple as that. Wimps.

It actually happened to me in Italy while sitting on the stairs on Loggia del Capitanato in my own Vicenza, 18 years ago. A drunk Muslim Moroccan man was objecting loudly about the fact that I was holding hands with my girlfriend at the time.

I felt like smacking him. And I could've right there and then, if he hadn't moved away. He was trying to impose his values on mine, in my own turf. Difficult topic. Who decides what the mores, the customs are? The people who've lived there the longest?

Well, here in India I can't do that. And I comply.

I am, however, more than puzzled, as I walk down the beach daily and I see the customary *gentil cacatore*, the kind defecator, digging his hole in the sand, waiting for me to pass by, and squatting down to show his private parts, his toxic debris exiting his orifice, then washing his intimate regions and walking away as if nothing happened.

Fine. *No problemo*. I realize it's perfectly ok here. And yet, after so many years, I still can't wrap my head around this sense of aesthetics.

I am so much less offended when I see a couple digging each other's mouth with their tongues. I can see it's not pretty, unless you're doing it. But it's prettier than public defecation, in my cultural mode. I'm a cheese-ball so I find it romantic, actually.

Anti-PDA brigades and kiss-vigilantes will publicly whip you, especially on St Valentine's day, if they catch you doing that, but I've never seen nor heard about even a single person getting hit for pissing on a wall or taking a crap on the side of the road. And I feel like doing that when I see them. Smack 'em on the head and yell 'Swacch Bharat, dude!' Clean India, man. Not 'Pissed on, India', not 'Shat on, India'. Love the Mother, right? If India is your mother, don't piss on it!

Men holding hands is ok. Because they don't know that in the gay community this is called homosocial behaviour. A gateway behaviour to homosexual love.

They might not like it, those RSS-prone youth. They think it's a show of fondness among friends, common also in many countries of the Mediterranean Sea. Although to most Western eyes it looks like homosocial venting of the need for intimacy with a loved one, since heterosexual effusions are punished and frowned upon.

What's more difficult, today? Being a man or being a woman in India? I think of a revealing anecdote told to me by a talented 20-something friend who lives in Delhi.

Akanksha said that while Uber-ing she often swipes

right six times, while standing on a deserted street, somewhere between Khan Market and Nizamuddin. She says she rejects drivers based on how menacing they look in their photograph in the app. I tell her she's confusing Uber with Tinder.

'Yeah, right. Look, once I came out of my apartment very late at night to catch my ride and I see this man leaning on his car with one arm straight, hips jutting out towards me, he was sucking on a lollipop, looking straight at me with dark bedroom eyes. So I said: Wait... and you are supposed to be my driver? You? Really? No, no, no, I don't think so, I said, and turned immediately on my heels to run back to my apartment.'

The problem is that after you reject a ride with Uber six times, you can't call a cab with the app for another hour. You are put in a sort of rejection quarantine until 60 minutes have passed.

If you are a 25-year-old girl in Delhi, even in a central area, this is not the ideal context. But this is one of the many new conundrums of a vastly technologized society, where Tinder habits (swipe right—reject!) are over-imposed on Uber habits (cancel the ride).

What's life like for a middle class 40-year-old divorced woman in India? How about a woman who doesn't want to have children although she's married? What has changed and how does it cohabit with the traditional attitude towards the body and its expression?

Thank god this is not an India book, so I will not even attempt to answer these questions.

I know that there have been, historically, many powerful women in India. I know the US still has not had a woman president. Spain, France, Italy never had a woman prime minister either. Italy still hasn't had even a woman as editor-in-chief of any major national daily newspaper for that matter.

I know about Indira Gandhi and Sonia Gandhi, and chief ministers Mamata and Mayawati and our very own Tamil Nadu's Jayalalitha. Does it matter that Amma Jayalalitha, the Bat-woman wearing a bulletproof cape, reached power by being the lover of the previous governor, MGR? Not really. Women will do what they have to in different historical periods.

I've met the matrilineal bosses of the Khasi tribes in Shillong. And the unfortunate leaders of the 'let's get back to patrilineal' movement. I've spent days with the matriarchal ladies of Nazaré, the last matriarchal society in Europe, a quaint little fishermen village on the coast of Portugal, and I've seen the rough ways in which the matriarchal ladies of Tuxla Gutierrez, in Mexico, handle their disobeying men. And I see daily in the mannerism and pride of Tamil women that activist and philosopher Periyar's early feminist battles were not useless at all.

Indian women have changed in the eyes of the world, lately. Hitting records. Now Indian women are leading, alongside the ladies of Venezuela, with the highest number of Miss World and Miss Universe winners.

And just consider that a few years ago a new category popped up in the free-porno Internet channels like YouPorn or PornHub. Yes, you guessed it: Indian women. There are even new sexual fantasy cartoons in the erotic web, a character called Velamma, a naughty, plump and sensual auntie getting busy in all the various Kamasutra poses with all kinds of people, for example. What does this say about global sexual fantasies, and about some reverse colonization happening in Western minds?

Indian women—to paraphrase the title of my wife's collection of poetry—are coming out of the woods.

So, women are set on a course.

It's the Indian men who are in trouble, because they are the ones who are forced to change the most, who must give up some abusive, comfortable power. The judges, editors-in-chief, powerful men who get caught with their hands up some girl's crotch. And they can't do it any more. Or not as often.

They are the ones most confused.

They are the ones who should be most interested in their future in India.

THE FUTURE OF INDIA!

Yes, all caps

This morning I set out for my early walk with the thought of going over, in my mind, the final chapter I'm supposed to write: 'THE FUTURE OF INDIA!' (yes, all caps, futurology is always screaming in terror or in misplaced enthusiasm).

A few minutes into my walk I run into a familiar scene. On the beach, 20 fishermen are drawing in a massive net. There are two queues, 100 metres from each other, pulling separate ends of a sharp plastic rope that disappear in the water.

Further away, in the village up the coast, another dozen fishermen are thrusting net-heavy fishing boats into the Bay, in this isolated corner of the world I've had the fortune of ending up in—a narrow isthmus between the Buckingham Canal and the Bay of Bengal, a spit of land between two bodies of water that is still mostly virginal and unbuilt.

As I look out into the horizon, I see trawlers and, here, listen, you can hear them, the smaller fishing boats' engine sound is pulsating like a heart beneath the splash of the waves.

The sun rises above us, as if birthed from the sea. I lose my gaze staring upon the glassy surface, which the wind ripples into a million reflections.

I always think, when I see these fishermen, my neighbours, my unknown beach companions beckoning me with their waving hands to join them and haul, I consider, observing them as they slowly tug on that long rope coming out of the sea, that they are pulling the sun up into the sky every morning, mythological icon of humanity bringing illusion into existence every day.

What will India fish out of the waters of the future? What is the future of India? What awaits India in the next decade? What are the premises, given the reality explored in this book? Will New India rise again? If so, how? What are the chances of India's future improving in the coming decade and what are the odds that it will actually regress into a traditionalist, close-minded mentality which will not promote the economy and thus the welfare of the majority of its citizens?

Well, thanks to Ganesh, Shiva, Parvati, Vishnu, Brahma, Hanuman, and Indra this...is...NOT...an... India...book!

So, I will not cite statistical studies about the future of India; neither probabilities nor guesses. I will not attempt a prediction about where it's heading, nor lure you with the most popular of products, the lyrical promises of a brilliant future.

Finally, I am just a vellai. I'm that stupid vellai with that stupid military cap with that stupid camera phone in his stupid hands snapping stupid photos of fishermen doing daily work, sweating under towel-turbans wrapped around their heads to protect them from the morning dampness of this Tamil Nadu February dawn. And who dares to be rude if someone wants to click a picture of him!

I'm that stupid vellai who shared with you his odd vellai observations. Like the fact that nets, in modern booming India, are still being pulled up by hand every morning on the beaches of Tamil Nadu. In 2018.

Or that, a world away from the Virtual Reality parlours of Bangalore, boats are still being pulled by hand into the waters, and automation is still waiting, patiently, to happen.

I was invited, once, to join a think tank organized by Tandem Research and the International Labour Organisation in a charming Portuguese colonial setting in Goa. Here, luminaries, experts, marketing geniuses, eminent professors and I gathered around a long table, under lazy slow fans, discussing how automation could destroy the future job market in India.

I underlined the simple evidence that the AC was not working, which, to me, seemed as eloquent an indication on the future of automation in India as any I could imagine. The machines may arrive. They'll break down often.

Once, sitting on the veranda, drinks in hand, I asked my father-in-law, Vinod, his opinion on the threat of automation as a job-killer.

He gave me good wisdom: 'You know, Carlo, yes, robots in India…ok. I run a business here, a factory, and we have machines that are constantly breaking down, we are constantly repairing them and maintaining them. So…robots? Bring them on! India will break them down to gears and wires!'

Especially southern India with the punishing nature of the heat. Come on, robots, we can take you on! The iodine and the salt in our seas will erode all your rubber parts, the metal will be slowly devoured by corrosion, by rust.

You will stop in mid-motion, crushed by Surya the Sun God, pulled out daily from the sea by the fishermen in Tamil Nadu.

Robots, you will be destroyed by thunderous Rudra, avatar of Shiva who annihilates the illusion of this reality!

Come on, robots, the future of India is awaiting you.

What else awaits in the future?

I can speak of what I see around me.

For example, something needs to be done, soon and fast, about the relationship with nature, about the poisonous burning rubber trash on my beach, upwind, by the probably underpaid servants of our probably too rich neighbours, in the Abbottabad bunker next door.

Something needs to be done about prohibiting the building of rock barriers on the beaches of the Bay of

Bengal, which cause immediate erosion south of the barriers, as it is happening, now, in front of my eyes, where a derelict huge trawler has washed up on the shores and in three months no one has been able to pull it out yet, although they keep trying. They tear a little piece at a time, waiting for nature, the sea, to do part of the job, and slowly chipping away some debris. Nature and men, working together, slowly. Quaint, but not as efficient as it could be.

In the future of India, no one should build new coal plants, as is being planned a few km from Arlanymor, south of here, indifferent to the destruction of the fantastic biodiversity thriving in the mangroves and jungles between the ocean and Marakkanam Lake.

Something needs to be done about securing the Kalpakkam nuclear power plant half an hour north of here, proving publicly that it really is not dangerous and that it is indeed secure, as it's claimed, against any accident that may or may not happen, just like they could or could not happen in Fukushima, Japan. And they did.

There are now 119 billionaires in India. The Bollygarchs. Collective worth: 440 billion US dollars. The average person in India earns barely 1,700 dollars a year. India remains a poor country. Proceeds of growth flow unusually fast to the very top, facilitated by global indifference to this inequality. In the future of India, someone needs to make sure that this growing Gross

Domestic Product, now the third largest in the world, is distributed more equally. Not less.

The fatalistic acceptance inspired by the ancient wisdom of the Vedas, kept alive in different forms, generation after generation, has tended to level out some of the useful social changes seasonally brought about in India. This is both good and bad.

Think of Gandhi's non-violence, or *ahimsa*, but then of the massacres of Muslims and Dalits. ('These days it is safer to be a cow than a Muslim in India,' parliamentarian Shashi Tharoor famously said.)

Think of B.R. Ambedkar's drive for equality and Dalit rights while drafting the Constitution, but then of caste politics today.

Think of Swami Vivekananda raising interfaith awareness while promoting Vedic thought throughout the world and look, now, at the popularity of Savarkar's hardline, divisive Hindutva stance.

In the paraphrased words of the very famous and overly quoted Italian novelist Giuseppe Tomasi di Lampedusa in *The Leopard*: 'If we want things to stay as they are, things will have to change.'

This is the story of Italy. This is the story of India. So in THE FUTURE OF INDIA there are more cycles of change, and of reactionary return to what was before. The samsara, game of illusion, cycles of history like games ricocheting through eternity.

We seem to be in a sort of undertow right now. Going back into the sea. Returning to certain fundamentalist stances: prohibiting people from holding hands in public, for example, while the economy grows, and with it, the dreams of entrepreneurs itching to leave the call center mentality and join a real, promising industrial wave.

Because there is also hope, now. Lots of beautiful, shiny, shakti-drenched hope.

*

After watching India transform in these 10 years, I know that demonetization and the new GST tax system—a simplification of bureaucracy which appeared to most as more complicated—has created a lot of dissatisfaction and disappointment in some of these young men who deal, for example, in cement, real estate, transportation, fashion or technology.

They were hoping for breaks, a pro-business environment that would help them foster their dreams. And it's not taken place. Not nearly.

Now I see them everywhere, these millennials not naturally prone to complaints, worrying about business slowing down because of the 52 GST documents they have to produce every month for every shipment, if they have a transport business shipping goods from state to state in India. And all of this, when the arrival of GST was supposed to simplify things. Or I see Daimler and

Dannon slowing down their operations here. Not good signs for economic growth.

But, this is something that by the time you read, might be floating away into the past and have no meaning. The point is to look at the larger picture of THE FUTURE OF INDIA and see what can be changed in the present to make the future more promising.

Promises of the future…There's always a little carrot being dangled in front of the donkey, right? The thing that pushes us forward in this mad belief, or maybe wise belief, that some things can be improved. And some things can.

What can be improved to guarantee a better future of India?

What would that mean, conclusively?

It would mean that the next time Ammu doesn't feel well, or slips or gets hurt or is simply tired, will sit on a chair, not on the floor, will drink from a glass, not the metal cup. Will say she takes off for a few hours, as is her right, without having to make up creative personal health excuses.

It means that the women, who come along with the men to rip weeds out of the garden with their hands, get paid the same, not in a roundabout, secret way, while the husbands, brothers, uncles and sons are not looking, but that they get equal pay in front of the men, who accept it as the correct thing to do.

It means poor people benefiting from growth, since so many of them contribute to the improvement of India by carrying the burden of an unequal system it is believed will at some point become more equal.

So, the better future of India is connected to the capacity to induct everyone into the great party that we're hoping will lie ahead, the arrival of growth while maintaining social peace, this harmony that I always vaguely perceive, lying beyond the madness of traffic, beyond the noise in the restaurants and in the public places, the occasional riots and protests, often justified, sometimes manipulated.

This harmony is the great superiority Asia has to offer and India specifically has to offer, as quality of life, compared to the Western conflictual culture of competitive economics.

The future of India should include more people in the prospective bonanza ahead.

*

And what is in *my* future in India?

India has brought me a new balance. I faced the difficulties of life in the sticks, the proper sticks, the silent, dark wilderness of an isolated beach, among the fishermen and shepherds.

I feel less alone here, in front of the sea, than in a dizzy megalopolis like Delhi. Here, I'm closer to myself.

I went through the season of settling in with dog demographic growth out of control, not finding a way to avoid the mosquitos, fearing dengue and malaria daily, fighting rats, getting used to the heat in all seasons, the weeds cutting my soft Western feet, the sleepless nights in the hot breath of summer, the in-heat all night barking, the monsoon flooding cutting off electricity for two weeks, the cyclone ripping into the heart of the forests and cities, and on and on into the rough side of Indian life.

Yet I've found a new balance in this wilderness; got the dogs vaccinated and spayed; learned to manage the rats and mosquitos; tamed my fears of diseases; understood I had to avoid the sun in the daytime, create the right breeze, as I also caved into air conditioning my studio in order to work in the summer (the poetry is not gone, Chetan). And I began to welcome with joy the refreshing arrival of monsoon rain.

I found stability in this wilderness.

Although I'm aware stability is an illusion, it's such a pretty illusion that I'll go along with it.

I will pull the sun out of the sea every morning.

Change comes, and change in India often comes slowly.

My wife and I had expected fewer years of isolated bliss than we are getting. The real estate projects pushing on all sides, the Calm Waters, the Tranquil Beaches that promised to bring in hundreds of tourists every weekend have stalled, for the moment.

Luckily we've not had to entrench ourselves, as it often happens when the Urban crashes into the Rural. We're still mostly the only ones here full-time, on this beach—the two writers, weirdos herding their three mongrel dogs up and down the beach like fruitless sheep.

Our Arlanymor paradise has not been destroyed yet by the ogling eyes, the growing stink, the unescapable noise, allowing us to still experience this version of India.

Not really knowing much about the deep, real life of the neighbours feels more Indian than making friends with everyone, like those vellai tourists, the yoga-people smiling at all strangers.

Yes, two hearts in a swanky hut, into the dark night and under the starry skies. No, we're not really integrated, because we can't be, which is the most Indian truth I can experience here, acknowledging the real limits of the integration of diversity, as candidly as I can.

This is what I think about, as I walk all alone at dawn, this morning on Bagheera beach. Paramankeni life, Arlanymor life.

The three dogs, Buggy, Bagheera, and Zelda are rummaging their wet noses through some rubbish that washed up last night, a Korean meditator is doing push-up yoga on the terrace of the Ashram while wearing his black sunglasses, four more are shooting phone photos of yoga poses, while the watchman lazily swings his baton eyeing the dogs and a fisherman pulls up his lungi, scuttling back to the village.

I love it here. I close my eyes, letting the light of dawn filter red through my eyelids. I open them again and feel like that sun burning in the sky is now expanding in my forehead, filling my throat and exploding morning joy into my chest.

I once was lost, when I first came here, and through yoga and meditation at first, through my struggles with learning the codes of a different culture, learning to eat and drive and party and manage bureau-crazy and bribe and smile like an Indian, I was slowly found.

My wife opened the doors of this paradise where we stroll together, remembering also how to walk alone.

I learned to accept a lot, to be patient, to let things happen, while trying my best.

I was given the greatest gift of tranquility by Mother India.

And even though I know one day I'm destined to lose it, because loss is a law of nature, in these 10 years I've let this calming, wild India grow inside me.

May it never leave me.

Bibliography

Bulgakov, Mikhail, *Heart of a Dog*, Harcourt, 2009.

Hesse, Herman, *Narcissus and Goldmund*, Fischer Verlag, 1930.

Kapur, Akash, *India Becoming*, Riverhead Books, 2012.

Keyserling, Count Herman, *The Travel Diary of a Philosopher*, Harcourt Brace, 1929.

Khilnani, Sunil, *Incarnations: India in 50 Lives*, Allen Lane, 2016.

Lampedusa, Giuseppe Tomasi di, *The Leopard*, Penguin Random House, 1960.

Mander, Harsh, *Looking Away*, Speaking Tiger, 2015.

Manganelli, Giorgio, *Esperimento con l'India*, Adelphi, 1992.

Nagarkar, Kiran, *The Extras*, Harper Collins, 2011.

Pratt, Hugo, *Corto Maltese: una ballata del mare salato*, Rizzoli Lizard, 1976.

Acknowledgements

I would like to thank my in-laws, Vinod and Eira Doshi, for welcoming me into their family with great love and generosity.

Special thanks to Eli Gottlieb for the constant encouragement and intelligent editing through many books and for insisting I write this one. Also thanks to Harri Krishnan, for his honesty and affection, to Maurizio Molinari for giving me the freedom to bring out my best and to my brother, Lodovico Pizzati, for being my first listener of storytelling.

I'd also like to acknowledge the conversations and collaborations with the following friends: William Dalrymple, Pankaj Mishra, Naresh Fernandes, Professor Gary Weaver, Sadanand Menon, Michael Wiegers, Fulvio Abbate, Daria Bignardi, Nicola Panciera, Fabrizio Andreella, Shekar Dattatri, Akanksha Sharma, Vikrom Mathur and Tandem Research.

I am also grateful to Dana Prescott and the Civitella Ranieri Foundation, and to Jason Gathorne-Hardy and the White House Farm Residency in Great Glemham, Suffolk, for their generous hospitality while writing and editing this book.